The 500 Hidden Secrets of

LISBON

INTRODUCTION

Lisbon has a rich history of more than 1000 years. It was one of the first truly global cities in the world, and thrived enormously during the Age of Discovery. But today it's also Europe's most vibrant and youthful capital. The city has found the perfect balance between those two identities: comfortable with both its heritage and the growing modernity, Lisbon breathes a radiant feel-good atmosphere, also much thanks to its colourful and poetic inhabitants.

Lisbon is so many things in one: it's a European capital but with the feel of a small rural village, with diverse and distinctive quarters; it's sophisticated and contemporary but also welcoming and easily accessible. It has beautiful hidden corners where time seems to stand still and fado music offers a mellow soundtrack, but it's also an increasingly popular food-and-wine destination, with many ethnic restaurants blending the influences of distant cultures and serving award-winning Portuguese wines. There are a million things to see and do, and even more to taste and savour.

This book will help you discover the soul of this remarkable city by guiding you to the 5 best places to meet people, or the 5 best restaurants to eat like a Portuguese. It tells you what you need to know about the 5 best Lisbon-area wines and the 5 most unique lifts and elevators – which are by the way very helpful in a city with so many hills.

HOW TO USE THIS BOOK?

This guide lists 500 things you need to know about Lisbon in 100 different categories. Most of these are places to visit, with practical information to help you find your way. Others are bits of information that help you get to know the city and its habitants. The aim of this guide is to inspire, not to cover the city from A to Z.

The places listed in the guide are given an address, including a district (for example Príncipe Real or Chiado), and a number. The district and number allow you to find the locations on the maps at the beginning of the book. Look for the map of the corresponding district, then look for the number. A word of caution however: these maps are not detailed enough to allow you to find specific locations in the city. A good map can be obtained from any tourist information centre or from most good hotels. Or the addresses can be located on a smartphone.

Please also bear in mind that cities change all the time. The chef who hits a high note one day can be uninspiring on the day you happen to visit. The hotel ecstatically reviewed in this book might suddenly go downhill under a new manager. The bar considered one of the 5 best places for live music might be empty on the night you visit. This is obviously a highly personal selection. You might not always agree with it. If you want to leave a comment, recommend a bar or reveal your favourite secret place, you can contact the publisher at *info@lusterweb.com*. Or follow *@500hiddensecrets* on Instagram and leave a comment – you'll also find free tips and the latest news about the series there.

THE AUTHOR

Born and bred Lisboeta Miguel Júdice is a hospitality entrepreneur and a passionate restaurateur. He is also the former president of the Portuguese Hotel Association, a freelance writer, a photographer, an amateur chef and an avid globetrotter. However Miguel always comes home to Lisboa. From the savvy Liberdade area to the bohemian Bairro Alto district, from the humble Belém neighbourhood to authentic Alfama: Miguel knows his away around all of Lisbon's secret places, and he is familiar with the city's people and traditions. You'll find him having coffee on a Chiado terrace, enjoying after-work drinks with friends in Príncipe Real, or walking around the historical Alfama district with his camera in hand, ready to capture images of the daily life of other locals.

More than visiting the most important sights, Miguel strongly recommends you to experience the daily life in Lisbon. Venture through the labyrinth-like quarters and enjoy getting lost. Sense the diversity of the cultures and the people that bring the city to life. Enjoy the views from the many riverside terraces. Go treasure and bargain hunting in Feira da Ladra or at other flea markets around town. Visit Lisbon's lush gardens and feast on local pastries and drinks. And, most of all, engage a conversation with the warm-hearted and friendly locals: you will be pleasantly surprised by their genuine kindness and their eagerness to talk about their city. You'll always end up with insightful suggestions of things to see and do, and you'll probably make new friends, with whom you can share laughs, stories, *petiscos* and drinks.

LISBON

overview

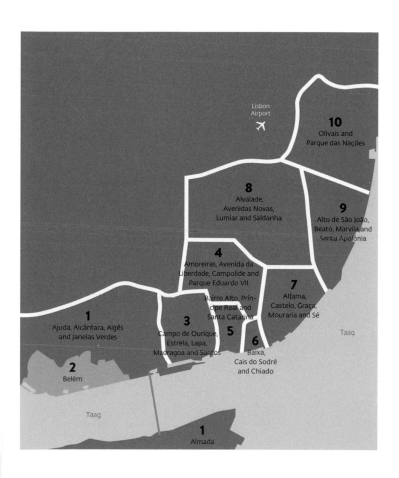

Lisbon
Airport

10
Olivais and
Parque das Nações

8
Alvalade,
Avenidas Novas,
Lumiar and Saldanha

9
Alto de São João,
Beato, Marvila and
Santa Apolónia

4
Amoreiras, Avenida da
Liberdade, Campolide and
Parque Eduardo VII

Bairro Alto, Prín-
cipe Real and
Santa Catarina

7
Alfama,
Castelo, Graça,
Mouraria and Sé

1
Ajuda, Alcântara, Algés
and Janelas Verdes

3
Campo de Ourique,
Estrela, Lapa,
Madragoa and Santos

5

6
Baixa,
Cais do Sodré
and Chiado

Taag

2
Belém

Taag

1
Almada

Map 1
AJUDA, ALCÂNTARA, ALGÉS,
ALMADA *and* JANELAS VERDES

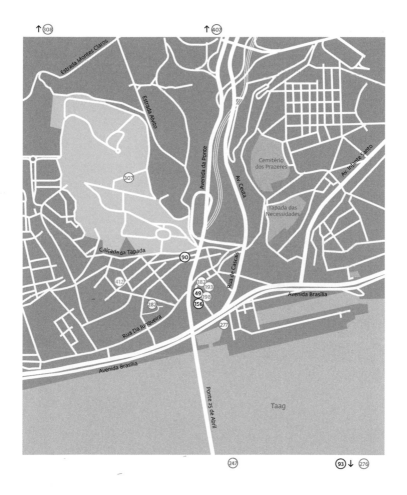

Map 2
BELÉM

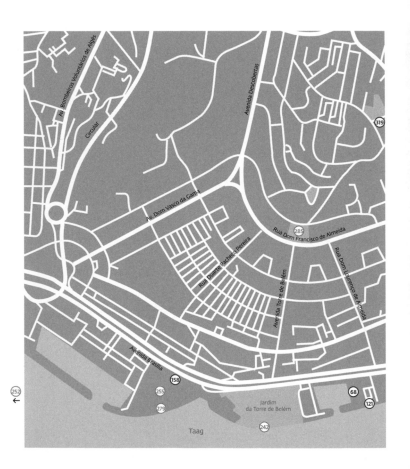

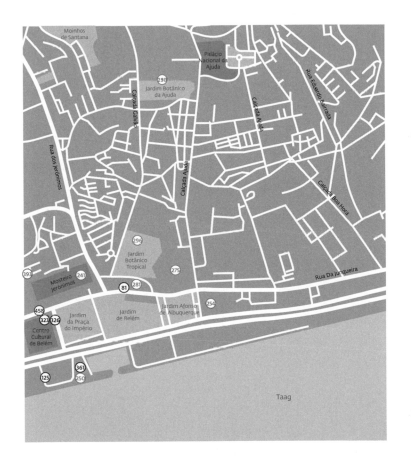

Map 3

CAMPO DE OURIQUE, ESTRELA, LAPA, MADRAGOA *and* SANTOS

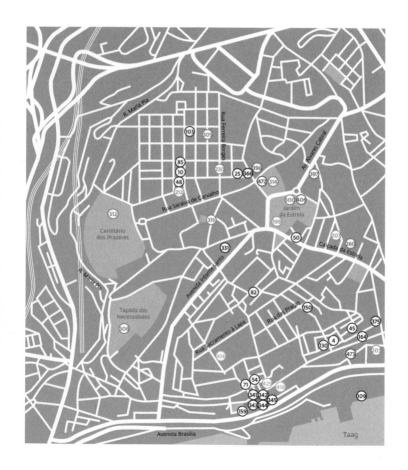

Map 4

AVENIDA DA LIBERDADE, AMOREIRAS, CAMPOLIDE *and* PARQUE EDUARDO VII

Map 5

BAIRRO ALTO, PRÍNCIPE REAL
and SANTA CATARINA

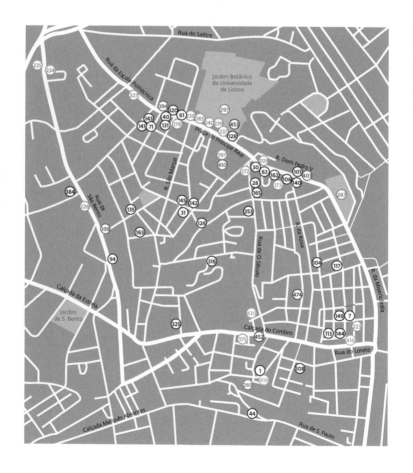

Map 6

BAIXA, CAIS DO SODRÉ
and CHIADO

Map 7

ALFAMA, CASTELO, GRAÇA, MOURARIA *and* SÉ

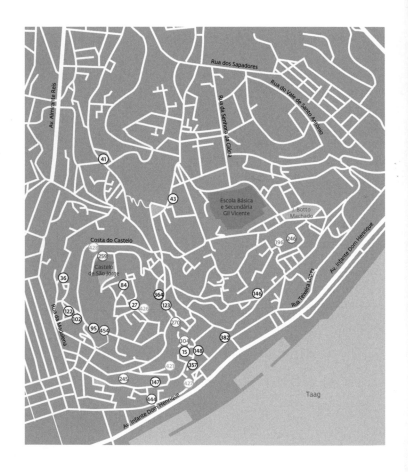

Map 8

ALVALADE, AVENIDAS NOVAS, LUMIAR and SALDANHA

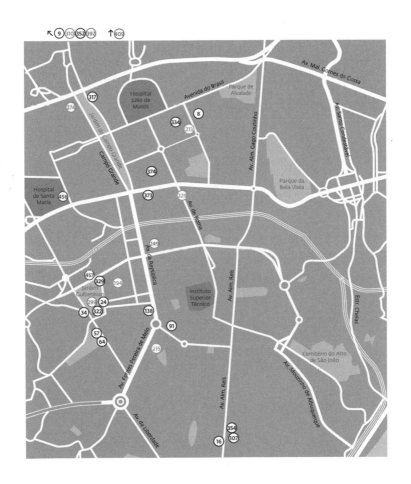

Map 9
ALTO DE SÃO JOÃO, BEATO, MARVILA *and* SANTA APOLÓNIA

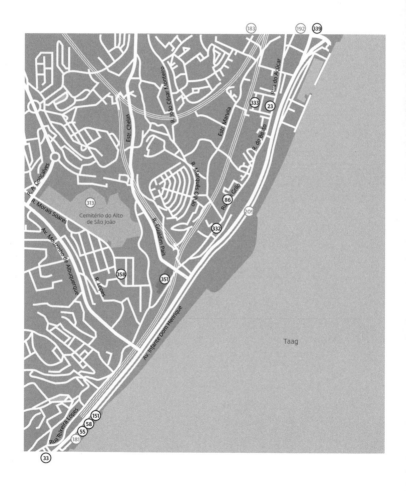

Map 10

OLIVAIS *and*

PARQUE DAS NAÇÕES

CEVICHERIA

105 PLACES TO EAT OR BUY GOOD FOOD

The 5 most
STUNNING
RESTAURANTS

---

1 **PHARMACIA**
Rua Marechal
Saldanha 1
Santa Catarina ⑤
+351 21 346 2146

Located in the Museum of Pharmacy, everything in this unique restaurant is connected to the theme of the old pharmacies. The comfort food menu, created by chef-owner Susana Felicidade, is pure bliss on a plate. There's also a great terrace overlooking the charming square of Santa Catarina.

2 **CASA DE PASTO**
Rua de São Paulo 20
1° andar
Cais do Sodré ⑥
+351 96 373 9979
www.casadepasto.com

A cool restaurant in one of the city's hippest neighbourhoods for foodies. The dishes on the menu are innovative but rustic at the same time. They're the perfect match for the very original décor that mirrors, in a intentionally kitsch way, the style of the traditional Portuguese homes.

3 **TAVARES**
Rua da
Misericórdia 35
Chiado ⑥
+351 21 342 1112
www.restaurante
tavares.net

It is the country's oldest surviving establishment, dating from 1784, and it has a tradition of serving classical cuisine, with a French inspiration. The eye-catching dining-room is decorated with gilded woodworks and stuccoes, chandeliers and mirrors.

4 **TRAVESSA**
Tv. do Convento das Bernardas 12
Madragoa ③
+351 21 394 0800
www.atravessa.com

Owned by Antonio and Viviane, a Portuguese-Belgian duo, Travessa has kept its allure and charm for over two decades. Located in an old convent in the heart of traditional Madragoa, the restaurant attracts a mixed crowd of local jet-setters and foreigners who come for the comfort food and great service.

5 **JNCQUOI**
Av. da Liberdade 182-184
Av. da Liberdade ④
+351 21 936 9900
www.jncquoi.com

This new addition to the Lisbon food (and shop and bar) scene has a very sophisticated look-and-feel, and blends in perfectly on the fashionable Avenida da Liberdade. In a cool setting, dominated by a replica of a dinosaur skeleton, you can have a light meal in the bar section, or taste innovative Portuguese cuisine in the restaurant.

3　TAVARES

The 5 best restaurants to
EAT LIKE A LOCAL

---

6 **STOP DO BAIRRO**
**Rua Marquês de
Fronteira 173-A
Campolide** ④
+351 21 585 2893

After many years in Campo de Ourique, Stop do Bairro moved to the next quarter. This place is famous with locals, who go there for the warm Portuguese food, very decent prices, and down-to-earth atmosphere. The restaurant is small, always full and you are likely to become friends with the patrons sitting next to you.

7 **PRIMAVERA
DO JERÓNIMO**
**Tv. da Espera 34
Bairro Alto** ⑤
+351 21 342 0477

The walls here are covered with photos of famous people who visited this small and simple restaurant in Bairro Alto, like Josephine Baker, to name one. The food is cooked in a traditional style, giving Primavera a homely feel that is part of the reason why it has been around for so long.

8 **SALSA & COENTROS**
**Rua Coronel
Marques Leitão 12
Alvalade** ⑧
+351 21 841 0990
www.salsaecoentros.pt

Salsa & Coentros is located near the airport, a bit off the beaten track and away from the areas where foreigners tend to stay and go out for food, but it is well worth the visit. This is one of the most awarded restaurants in the city, famous for the traditional food from the region of Alentejo.

9 **GALITO**
Rua Adelaide
Cabete 7
Lumiar ⑧
+351 21 711 1088

Thé place to try traditional dishes from the Alentejo region is Galito. It is one of those restaurants where you really feel the presence and warmth of the owners, who tend to the kitchen and to the service as well. The walls are lined with clippings from decades of positive media reviews. Go for the Sopa de Cação and the lamb dishes.

10 **PARREIRINHA DO MINHO**
Rua Francisco
Metrass 47-49
Campo de Ourique ③
+351 21 396 9028

This is where you go for perfectly grilled fish and meat. It is a warm, family-owned, neighbourhood restaurant that caters mainly to locals, some of whom dine here every week.

The 5 best
restaurants with a cool
LISBON ATMOSPHERE

---

11 **100 MANEIRAS**
Largo da Trindade 9
Chiado ⑥
+351 91 030 7575
www.restaurante
100maneiras.com

100 Maneiras is owned by Ljubomir Stanisic, a Sarajevo-born and Belgrade-raised chef. The atmosphere is one of the best in town and the food lives up to the expectations as well, with dishes inspired by the culinary traditions of Portugal, France and Yugoslavia, but with a daring twist. It's the trademark of Ljubomir, who refuses to feel inhibited out of respect for the past.

12 **MINI BAR**
Rua António Maria
Cardoso 58
Chiado ⑥
+351 21 130 5393
www.minibar.pt

Star chef José Avillez opened this gastropub in a former theatre around the corner from his two-Michelin-star restaurant Belcanto. At Mini Bar the menu is filled with Portuguese-style tapas. The décor echoes the building's theatrical past and is informal and sophisticated at the same time.

13 TABERNA MODERNA

Rua dos Bacalhoeiros 18A
Baixa ⑥
+351 21 886 5039
www.taberna moderna.com

Located on the edge of Alfama, Taberna Moderna is literally what the name means in Portuguese, namely a modern tavern. The owners were inspired by the traditional small restaurants that you find all over the city, but they added a contemporary touch to the concept.

14 THE DECADENTE

Rua de São Pedro de Alcântara 81
Chiado ⑥
+351 21 346 1381
www.thedecadente.pt

The brainchild of the Eça Leal brothers, The Decadente is attached to their award-winning hostel. This is one of the city's hotspots, with an eclectic vibe and an international crowd, which ensures a great atmosphere every single night.

15 SANTO ANTÓNIO DE ALFAMA

Beco de São Miguel 7
Alfama ⑦
+351 21 888 1328
www.siteantonio.com

This three-storey restaurant has an amazing location. Try to get a table on the exceptional outdoor terrace (first come, first serve), set in a small alley covered with grapevines, where local residents go about their lives in the adjoining houses.

14 THE DECADENTE

The 5 best restaurants for
FISH AND SEAFOOD

---

16 **RAMIRO**

Avenida Almirante Reis 1 - H
Baixa ⑧
+351 21 885 1024
www.cervejaria ramiro.pt

Lisbon's most famous seafood restaurant Ramiro has been around for half a century now, attracting food loving crowds from all over the world. The quality of the fish and seafood served here is absolutely superior – everything is caught daily in the cold Atlantic waters and cooked to sheer perfection. Book ahead as this restaurant gets full every night.

17 **SEA ME**

Rua do Loreto 21
Chiado ⑥
+351 21 346 1564
www.peixaria moderna.com

Sea Me calls itself a 'modern fish market' where you can eat and/or buy fish and seafood. A selection of what's on offer comes straight from the on site salt-water tanks with live shellfish. In the restaurant the food ranges from local specialties to sushi made with the fresh fish on offer.

18 IBO MARISQUEIRA

**Rua da Cintura
do Porto 22
Cais do Sodré ⑥
+351 21 342 3611
www.ibo-
restaurante.pt**

A former salt warehouse by the river houses one the most unique restaurants in town. The food is inspired by the cuisine of former Portuguese colony Mozambique, with some influences from Goa (India) blended in. Try the scallops, the biggest and tastiest you will ever see.

19 AQUI HÁ PEIXE

**Rua da Trindade 18A
Chiado ⑥
+351 21 343 2154
www.aquihapeixe.pt**

At Aqui há Peixe you are sure to find prime quality fish on offer, grilled to perfection by chef Miguel Reino. He and his wife Mafalda also own the place. They are experienced jet-set restaurateurs with an enthusiastic crowd of fans who followed after they moved their business from the hippie-chic Pego beach in Comporta to Chiado.

20 MARISQUEIRA AZUL

**Mercado da Ribeira,
Av. 24 de Julho 49
Cais do Sodré ⑥
+351 21 131 8599**

This restaurant in the outdoor wing of Mercado da Ribeira sits right next to the fish stands that sell the best and freshest seafood in town, so you can be assured that the quality of the products here is first rate. The hip and urban look-and-feel is very different from your typical seafood-restaurant-atmosphere.

The 5 best
A S I A N
restaurants

---

21 CAXEMIRA
Rua Condes de
Monsanto 4
Baixa ①
+351 21 886 5486

This is a great option for those who like Indian cuisine. Located on a first floor of Praça da Figueira, Caxemira is hard to find and also hard to get a table at, so do book one in advance. The restaurant is famous for traditional dishes like samosas and shrimp curry with coconut sauce. For dessert try the *bebinca*.

22 BOA BAO
Largo Rafael Bordalo
Pinheiro 30
Chiado ⑥
+351 91 902 3030
www.boabao.pt

Boa Bao hit Lisbon like an earthquake when it opened in early 2017. Gregg Hupert and his wife Nathalie brought a very strong concept to the city, and paid great attention to every little detail in the design. The lines of people waiting outside speak for themselves: the locals love this place and the quality of the Pan-Asian food that's served.

23 DINASTIA TANG

Rua do Açúcar 107
Beato ⑨
+351 21 812 3349
www.restaurante-
chines.com

Located in an old wine warehouse in the up-and-coming Beato district, Dinastia Tang is a truly outstanding restaurant that serves genuine Chinese cuisine from the region of Canton. The magical setting takes you back to the Ming and Tang dynasties.

24 GO JUU

Rua Marquês Sá da
Bandeira 46
Avenidas Novas ⑧
+351 21 828 0704

Go Juu started as a private club for sushi lovers: only members and their friends were allowed. Gradually the restaurant started opening up to non-members and now it welcomes all sushi-lovers, who flock to this less touristic area of the city to savour what's probably the best Japanese food in Lisbon.

25 TABERNA JAPONESA

Rua Coelho
da Rocha 20-A
Campo de Ourique ③
+351 21 395 5555

Formerly the head sushi chef at Yakuza, Aguinaldo Silva decided to venture out on his own and opened a Japanese tavern in the quarter of Campo de Ourique. Here you sit at a wooden counter to enjoy the fantastic sushi and sashimi. Try the scrumptious black cod with pickled ginger sprouts.

The 5 best
SMALL RESTAURANTS

---

26 **TABERNA DA RUA DAS FLORES**
Rua das Flores 103
Chiado ⑥
+351 21 347 9418

There's a constant line of people waiting outside this restaurant, and here's why: they don't take reservations here, the restaurant is small, the food is delicious and very good value. Owned by self-taught chef André Magalhães, this tiny temple of traditional cuisine mirrors the old *tabernas* of Lisbon in both the décor and the food served.

27 **LEOPOLD**
Pátio de Dom Fradique 12
Castelo ⑦
+351 21 886 1697

Good news: this once extremely tiny restaurant moved from Mouraria to Palácio Belmonte in the Castelo quarter, where there's a bit more space for a few extra tables, so now more patrons have the chance to taste the exquisite dishes of chef-owner Tiago Feio. His cuisine is clean, delicate, innovative and he has a great eye for presentation.

28 LOCAL

Rua de O Século 204
Príncipe Real ⑤
+351 92 567 5990

At Local, some of the city's younger chefs cook side by side in an 18-square-metre one table (seats 10 people) restaurant. Food is prepared as you look on. The restaurant is tucked away on a quiet street in Príncipe Real. Rua on the opposite side of the street is also a good spot.

29 KANAZAWA

R. Damião
de Góis 3-A
Algés ①
www.kanazawa.pt

Japanese Chef Tomoaki Kanazawa, who also ownes the celebrated restaurant Tomo, opened this small, exclusive, eight-seat restaurant in Algés. He then moved back to Japan and handed the reigns over to Paulo Morais, Portugal's leading Asian food chef. The set menu takes you on a journey through the *kaizeki* cuisine, with dozens of highly creative, dazzling dishes.

30 CEVICHERIA

R. Dom Pedro V 129
Príncipe Real ⑤
+351 21 803 8815
www.chefkiko.com

Owner and chef Kiko of Cevicheria is one of the new stars of the local food scene. His ceviches and tartares are so amazing that every day you will find people lining up on the street in front of his restaurant, hoping to get a highly coveted table inside, while drinking their killer Pisco Sours.

The 5 best places for
BURGERS

---

31 HONORATO

Rua da Palmeira 33A
Príncipe Real ⑤
+351 21 346 0248
www.honorato.pt

Today Honorato is one of the largest burger chains in Portugal, with branches in Lisbon and elsewhere. But, like McDonald's, Honorato started out small, with one restaurant in Príncipe Real, where burger master Márcio Honorato worked his magic and created icons like the X-Tudo, Capitão Fausto and Troika.

32 HAMBURGUERIA DO BAIRRO

Rua Ilha dos Amores 4
Parque das Nações ⑩
+351 21 894 1175
*www.hamburgueria
dobairro.com*

Another of the city's burger chains, Hamburgueria do Bairro has branches in Príncipe Real, Santos, Restelo and Parque das Nações, each with its own feel. The menu boasts 11 different recipes, all made with 160 grams of prime quality beef, except for the one burger that's suitable for vegetarians of course; that one is prepared with tofu.

33 CAIS DA PEDRA

33 CAIS DA PEDRA

**Armazém B, loja 9,
Avenida Infante
Dom Henrique
Santa Apolónia ⑨
+351 21 887 1651
*www.caisdapedra.pt***

TV chef Henrique Sá Pessoa created this burger concept in a large old warehouse by the river. His partners also own the Honorato restaurants but the concepts are different, as the recipes of Cais da Pedra have been created by Henrique, who manages to add a touch of creativity and sophistication to minced meat.

34 GROUND BURGER

**Avenida António
Augusto de
Aguiar 148-A
Avenidas Novas ⑧
+351 21 371 7171
*www.ground
burger.com***

Tucked away on a small square next to the Gulbenkian Garden, this burger restaurant prides itself on its old school American burgers (homemade with Black Angus meat) and on a wide selection of craft beers. Try also the garlic and rosemary french fries and the crispy onion rings.

35 TO.B

**Rua Capelo 24
Chiado ⑥
+351 21 347 1046**

All burgers at To.B are made with meat from the Azores Islands, famous for their pollution-free grazing fields. The owner, Carlos Cortês, is a former executive at a large Portuguese conglomerate and is always on site to add a more personal note to the guests' experience.

The 5 best places for a
HEALTHY MEAL

36 **THE FOOD TEMPLE**
Beco do Jasmim 18
Mouraria ⑦
+351 21 887 4397
www.thefood
temple.com

Chef Alice Ming opened a vegan restaurant on a secluded, intimate and stunning dead end square in the decadent Mouraria district. The menu changes daily depending on what's on offer at the market but it is invariably full of heart and creative. Be sure to book a table and ask to be seated on the square steps for an even richer experience.

37 **TIBETANOS**
Rua do Salitre 117
Av. da Liberdade ④
+351 21 314 2038
www.tibetanos.com

This Tibetan-inspired restaurant is open for lunch and dinner and is a favourite among health-minded locals. It's one of the oldest veggie restaurants in the city and it is part of a cultural institution that includes a Buddhist school. The backyard terrace is a great option during warmer months.

38 MISS SAIGON

**Rua Cais das Naus
Parque das Nações** ⑩
+351 21 099 6589
www.miss-saigon.pt

Miss Saigon is a vegetarian restaurant that serves 'world vegetarian cuisine', with dishes inspired by the culinary traditions of both East and West. In 2015 Miss Saigon was named one of the 25 best vegetarian restaurants in the world by the website Daily Meal.

39 JARDIM DAS CEREJAS

**Calçada do
Sacramento 36
Chiado** ⑥
+351 21 346 9308
*www.jardim
dascerejas.com*

This intimate restaurant, located on a quiet street just off busy Rua Garrett, on the way to Largo do Carmo, offers a daily vegetarian buffet for a very good price. It's the favourite address of many international visitors.

40 NAKED

**Rua da Escola
Politécnica 85
Príncipe Real** ⑤
+351 93 482 5753
www.naked.com.pt

Located right across the street from the Museum of Natural History and the Botanical Garden, Naked is an all-day restaurant and café that serves masterfully prepared natural foods, with veggie and non-veggie options, raw, gluten-free, cold pressed juices and 100% fruit popsicles. The beautiful décor fits into the picture of the hip neighbourhood.

The 5 best places for

CHEAP EATS

---

41 COZINHA POPULAR DA MOURARIA
Rua das Olarias 5
Mouraria ⑦
+351 92 652 0568

This restaurant in Mouraria was created by photographer and cooking aficionada Adriana Freire, as part of a social project: Freire is committed to helping vulnerable people integrate by providing jobs for them at her restaurant. Calling it a restaurant doesn't quite cover the load actually – this place also serves as a community kitchen that residents can use as an operating base for their own small food businesses.

42 MARTIM MONIZ
Baixa ⑥

Martim Moniz is a 'fusion market' located on a square in downtown Lisbon. It consists of about a dozen kiosks offering food from around the world. It's also the place to be for many events that all aim to be an ode to and a celebration of the cultural diversity of this part of Lisbon.

43 BOTEQUIM DA GRAÇA

Largo da Graça 79-80
Graça ⑦
+351 21 888 8511
www.botequim.net

Botequim da Graça was founded in 1968 by famous writer Natália Correia and for decades it has been a meeting place for artists and intellectuals. There are poetry nights and live music, all set in a retro atmosphere that's created by the antiques-filled décor. On the menu you'll find Portuguese tapas.

44 PISTOLA Y CORAZÓN

Rua da Boavista 16
Cais do Sodré ⑤
+351 21 342 0482
www.pistola
ycorazon.com

This small *taqueria* (taco shop) is as genuine as it gets: the moment you walk through the doors, it feels as if you were in the heart of México City. It's a great place to enjoy good music and innovative cocktails, made mostly with tequila.

45 OSTERIA

Rua das
Madres 52-54
Madragoa ③
+351 21 396 0584
www.osteria.pt

Osteria is probably Lisbon's closest thing to a true Italian restaurant; it's owned by an Italian cook who prepares genuine Italian home-style dishes. The service is like the food: friendly, warm and easy-going.

The 5 best
CAKE SHOPS

---

46 NÓS É MAIS BOLOS
Mercado da Ribeira
Cais do Sodré ⑥
+351 21 346 0237
www.nosemais
bolos.com

This gourmet cake shop is located on the Mercado da Ribeira and offers a selection of the best cakes in Portugal, including traditional favourites like the *pão de ló* (sponge cake). It's a great option to go dessert hunting after a meal at one of the Mercado's food stalls.

47 LANDEAU CHOCOLATE
Rua das Flores 70
Chiado ⑥
+351 91 181 0801
www.landeau.pt

Sofia Landeau created and amazing chocolate cake which she now sells in her stores on Rua das Flores and at LX Factory. *The New York Times* called it 'devilishly good', others would rather call it a slice of heaven. It is moist and decadent as chocolate cakes should be, with a layer of soft cake and another of bitter chocolate mousse.

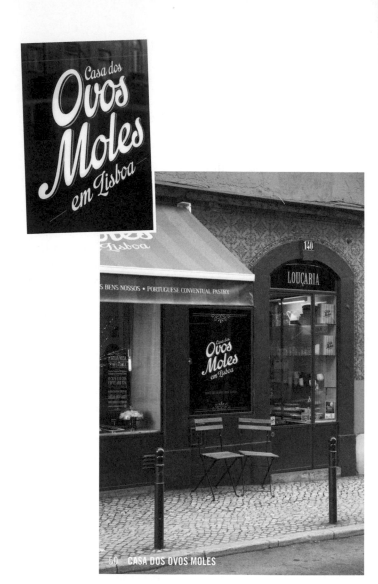

60 CASA DOS OVOS MOLES

48 MELHOR BOLO DE CHOCOLATE DO MUNDO

Rua Terente Ferreira
Durão 62
Campo de Ourique ③
+351 21 396 5372
www.omelhorbolode
chocolatedomundo
bycbl.com

Former restaurateur Carlos Brás Lopes created a delicious and decadently sweet chocolate cake and went on and called it 'The Best Chocolate Cake in the World'. Many agree and would even say that this cake is one of the best cakes you will ever find. In fact it's so good and so popular that Lopes opened shops in New York, London and São Paulo.

49 BOLO DA MARTA

LX Factory,
Livraria Ler Devagar,
R. Rodrigues Faria 103
Alcântara ①
+351 91 892 9654

Marta Gonçalves' highly successful cake business started out rather simple, with her baking her signature pavlova cake for friends' parties. Little by little she started getting more and more orders and that's when she realised that there was a career in baking. Her shop inside LX Factory's Ler Devagar bookshop is full of delicious temptations.

50 CASA DOS OVOS MOLES

Calçada da
Estrela 140-142
Estrela ③
+351 91 930 3788
www.casadosovos
molesemlisboa.pt

Portugal has a strong tradition of making and eating egg-based sweets, which finds its origin in the old days when the nuns in Portuguese convents used egg whites to starch their habits; with the leftover egg yolks they made sweets. If you would like to try these *ovos moles*, this small shop in Estrela in the place to be.

The 5 best places for a
SUNDAY BRUNCH

---

51 NICOLAU CAFÉ

Rua de São Nicolau 17
Baixa ⑥
+351 21 886 0312

Nicolau is a cool café/restaurant in one of the more quiet streets of otherwise busy Baixa. Its carefully designed interior and healthy menu, with for example smoothies and açai bowls, attract a hip crowd. The café doubles as the food and beverage outlet of the hostel that's located in the same building, and that's considered one of the best in the world.

52 ESTUFA REAL

Jardim Botânico
da Ajuda,
Calçada do Galvão
Ajuda ①
+351 21 361 9400
www.estufareal.com

When it comes to Sunday brunch, there's no place quite like Estufa Real. The setting is stunning: a converted greenhouse in the botanical garden of Ajuda, where guests can marvel at the breathtaking view of the river and where they can enjoy a kind of peacefulness that is rare to find in the city. The ample selection of cold and warm dishes more than justifies the somewhat higher prices.

53 GRÉMIO LITERÁRIO JAZZ BRUNCH

Rua Ivens 37
Chiado ⑥
+351 91 771 9447

Brunch at this one-of-a-kind place in Chiado is served on Saturdays. On that day the doors of Lisbon's most exclusive private club swing open to welcome guests into an atmosphere of Old World charm and sophistication. Dine in the veranda with a view of the river and the club's secret garden. The cherry on the cake is the live jazz music, making this an even more unique experience.

54 LA BOULANGERIE

Rua do Olival 42
Santos ③
+351 21 395 1208
laboulangerielisboa.
business.site

The location of La Boulangerie alone is worth the visit. This charming French-style bakery rises up above a serene square that overlooks the Ancient Art Museum. Weather permitting, brunch can be enjoyed outside on a terrace next to the circular fountain in the square. Don't miss their *pain au chocolat*…

55 BICA DO SAPATO

Av. Infante Dom
Henrique,
Arm. B, Cais da Pedra
Santa Apolónia ⑨
+351 21 881 0320
www.bica
dosapato.com

Bica do Sapato is owned by a group of restaurateurs and artists including John Malkovich. The location on the riverbank is quite unique, the décor is cosmopolitan. Sunday brunch is popular even among the most discerning Lisboetas.

The 5 best
FOOD SHOPS

---

56 SILVA & FEIJÓO
**Rua dos Bacal-
hoeiros 117
Baixa ⑥
+351 91 216 3084**

Occupying a stone-walled shop near Casa dos Bicos that dates from 1919, Silva & Feijóo sells a great selection of traditional products from all around Portugal and the islands of Madeira and Azores. The list includes farm bread, wine, liquors, cheese and smoked meats, and sausages.

57 CLUB DEL GOURMET
**Av. António Augusto
de Aguiar 31
Avenidas Novas ⑧
+351 21 371 1700
*www.elcorteingles.pt***

Located in the El Corte Inglès department store, this shop has more than 6000 food articles on offer, like smoked meats, canned food, pastas and olive oil. The wine listing boasts some hard to find labels and vintages. Very attentive and expert service.

58 DELI DELUX
**Av. Infante Dom
Henrique, Cais da
Pedro, Arm. B, loja 8
Santa Apolónia ⑨
+351 21 886 2070
*www.delidelux.pt***

Occupying a reconverted warehouse in Santa Apolónia, Deli Delux is a trendy delicatessen and cafe that has the best and biggest selection of all of Lisbon's foodstores. The cool cafe serves light meals using the products on sale and has an outside terrace offering breathtaking views of the Tagus river.

59 MERCEARIA DOS AÇORES
Rua da Madalena 115
Baixa ⑥
+351 21 888 0070
www.mercearia
dosacores.pt

The archipelago of the Azores is Portugal's most pristine and remote region. The rich Atlantic waters have the best fish in the country and the countryside is heaven for organic farming. Mercearia dos Açores sells products from this region exclusively, like pineapples, tuna, organic teas and high-quality dairy products.

60 CONSERVEIRA DE LISBOA/NACIONAL
Rua dos
Bacalhoeiros 34
Baixa ⑥
+351 21 886 4009
www.conserveira
delisboa.pt

Portugal has a strong tradition when it comes to *conservas* (canned food): the Portuguese have been producing and consuming it for generations and as a result, their canned foods are some of the best in the world. The industry's flagship is the shop of Conserveira Nacional, where you will find the biggest selection of brands and varieties – a true *conservas* museum if you will.

60 CONSERVEIRA DE LISBOA

The 5 best places to buy
CHEESE AND SMOKED MEATS

---

61 QUEIJARIA CHEESE SHOP
Rua do Monte Olivete 40
Príncipe Real ⑤
+351 21 346 0474
www.queijaria.wix.com/queijaria

Queijaria Cheese Shop aims to be the best place in town for discovering the richness and the variety of Portuguese artisanal cheeses. It's a place where cheese 'junkies' can feed their addiction and taste all kinds of cheeses over a glass of wine in the cheese bar.

62 MANTEIGARIA SILVA
Rua Dom Antão De Almada 1
Baixa ⑥
+351 21 342 4905
www.manteigaria silva.pt

Manteigaria Silva has been around since 1890 and the Silva family is still in charge of the business. At this Baixa shop you will find a selection of fine cheeses (some cured on site), smoked meats (sliced on a 100-year-old machine) and dry codfish from the North Sea.

63 MOY
Rua Dom Pedro V 111
Príncipe Real ④
+351 21 346 7011

Moy has two shops in Lisbon, one in Príncipe Real and another in Alvalade. Both offer a large selection of gourmet products, including some Portuguese cheeses like Serra, Azeitão, Ilha and Nisa. The expert staff will help you pick the perfect cheese, explaining its origins and production process.

64 **CINCO JOTAS**
Avenida António
Augusto de Aguiar 31
El Corte Inglês, Piso 7
Avenidas Novas ⑧
+351 21 371 1700

This shop is located on the top floor of the El Corte Inglès department store, and sells smoked meats from one of the world's top brands, Cinco Jotas. All meats are cured in the Jabugo region in Spain, where black pigs are raised for as long as five years in the wild eating acorns.

65 **QUEIJARIA NACIONAL**
Rua da Conceição 8
Baixa ⑥
+351 91 208 2450

Queijaria Nacional is a cheese specialty shop with the finest artisan cheeses on offer, all produced in different parts of Portugal. You can enjoy them on the premises accompanied by a glass of good wine and a slice of smoked meat. The shop is conveniently located in front of one of the stops of the famous 28 tram.

62 MANTEIGARIA SILVA

The best 5 restaurants for
EXCEPTIONAL
COOKING

---

66 **ELEVEN**
Jardim Amália
Rodrigues
Rua Marquês de
Fronteira
Parque Eduardo VII ④
+351 21 386 2211
www.restaurant
eleven.com

Eleven is located in Parque Eduardo VII, Lisbon's 'central park', offering an impressive view over the city and the river. The cuisine, awarded with one Michelin star, is the creation of chef Joachim Koerper, who works with only the best products that Portugal has to offer, especially fresh fish. The décor is fashionable and sophisticated.

67 **BELCANTO**
Largo de
São Carlos 10
Chiado ⑥
+351 21 342 0607
www.belcanto.pt

Located next to the Opera House, Belcanto is the crown jewel of celebrity chef José Avillez's restaurant group, and the only restaurant in town to have been granted two Michelin stars. The dishes are prepared with incredible skill, and the whole experience of dining there is quite entertaining and memorable.

68 **FEITORIA**
Altis Belém
Hotel & Spa
Doca do Bom Sucesso
Belém ②
+351 21 040 0207
www.restaurante
feitoria.com

At the helm of one-Michelin-star restaurant Feitoria, located in the Altis Belém Hotel, stands Chef João Fernandes, one of the country's youngest top chefs. His innovative dishes are served in a setting that pays tribute to the Portuguese discoveries of the 15th and 16th centuries.

69 **VARANDA**
Rua Rodrigo da
Fonseca 88
Parque Eduardo VII ④
+351 21 381 1400
www.fourseasons.com/
lisbon

Varanda is famous for the lunch buffet, making this the city's top power lunch spot. The food is amazing and so well presented you feel like taking pictures the whole time. The classic and perfect Four Seasons' service is the cherry on top of a delicious cake.

70 **ALMA**
Rua Anchieta 15
Chiado ⑥
+351 21 347 0650
www.almalisboa.pt

After having been kept in a stand-by modus for several years, the Alma concept by star chef Henrique Sá Pessoa was recently brought back to life, to the great delight of its many fans. The new location is a stone-arched building in Chiado. Here, Sá Pessoa lets his creativity run wild while creating a cuisine with lots of Portuguese soul (which is what *alma* means).

The 5 best places for
EXOTIC FOOD

---

71 COMIDA DE SANTO
Calçada Eng. Miguel Pais 39
Príncipe Real ⑤
+351 21 396 3339
www.comida desanto.pt

Here's one of the oldest ethnic restaurants in Lisbon. Its story dates back to the 80s, when it was the first restaurant to open in Príncipe Real, and it has had a loyal following ever since. Owners Tó Zé and Flor offer a service that is as warm, comforting and friendly as the traditional Brazilian food on their menu.

72 GEOGRAPHIA
Rua do Conde 1
Santos ③
+351 21 396 0036
www.restaurante geographia.pt

Geographia pays tribute to the richness of Portuguese gastronomy, one of the world's first fusion cuisines and a result of the influences that the Portuguese brought back from the 'worlds' we discovered. Likewise, the cuisine of Portuguese-speaking countries was influenced by Portuguese cuisine. The location is lovely, in a calm square that overlooks the National Ancient Art Museum.

73 JESUS É GOÊS

Rua de São José 23
Av. da Liberdade ④
+351 21 154 5812

Jesus is a larger than life chef who originally hails from Goa, a former Portuguese colony in India. The restaurant's name means 'Jesus is from Goa' – true as can be. The traditional Goan dishes he serves are spicy and authentic and a blend of local Goan ingredients and foods that were imported by the Portuguese.

74 ASSOCIAÇÃO CABOVERDEANA

Rua Duque de
Palmela 2, 8º
Av. da Liberdade ④
+351 21 359 3367
www.acabo
verdeana.org

This very well-kept secret is difficult to find as it is located on the top floor of an office building. The Associação Caboverdeana is in fact an institution that promotes the culture of Cabo Verde. And what better way is there to do so than by hosting a restaurant? It's open for lunch during the week, serving traditional cuisine to the sound of live African music.

75 SOL E PESCA

Rua Nova do
Carvalho 44
Cais do Sodré ⑥
+351 21 346 7203
www.solepesca.com

This former fishing equipment shop, where the décor has remained unchanged, now houses one of the most original bars/restaurants in Lisbon. Everything you can order here to eat is prepared exclusively with canned fish and seafood. Sit outside on the street for an even more unforgettable experience.

5 specialities to
EAT AND DRINK
BEFORE YOU LEAVE

---

76 GINJINHA

Ginjinha is a Portuguese liqueur and a typical alcoholic drink in Lisbon. You can find plenty of little kiosks selling it around the city, especially in the downtown area of Baixa. It is made by infusing sour cherries in alcohol and then adding sugar.

77 SARDINHAS

You simply cannot visit Lisbon and not eat sardines, especially if you come between April and October. Everywhere you go you smell these oily small fish (rich in vitamins and minerals), being grilled outdoors on the street in front of restaurants or in front of local homes. Beware of the thin bones, they can get stuck in the oddest places.

78 **CONSERVAS**

In the old days, before people had fridges, *conservas* were a way to preserve food. They were extremely popular and a major export product. Because of modernisation the industry took a downward fall and almost disappeared at a certain point. But, thanks to the 'back to basic' trend, *conservas* have become popular again in recent years and now you can find them in gourmet and souvenir shops around town.

79 **PASTÉIS DE NATA**

These are the most revered sweets in the city and you will find them in every cafe. The most famous are undoubtedly those from Belém, where they claim to have the original recipe. They are really delicious but do try other brands and stores to try to find the differences.

80 **CALDO VERDE**

Portugal calls itself a 'Soup Country' and *caldo verde* (green cabbage soup) is perhaps the country's soup jewel. It is a simple yet delicious soup, made with potato cream and shredded green cabbage. The final touch is a drop of extra virgin olive oil and a few slices of *chouriço* (smoked sausage).

The 5 best
PASTÉIS DE NATA

81 **PASTÉIS DE BELÉM**
Rua de Belém 84-92
Belém ②
+351 21 363 7423
www.pasteisdebelem.pt

The owners of Pastéis de Belém claim they have the original recipe for these popular sweets. According to tradition they could be right, as the recipe is said to have originated from the Jeronimos Monastery next door. Coming to Lisbon and not trying one is like going to Rome and not having pasta.

82 **PASTELARIA CRISTAL**
Rua Buenos Aires 25A
Lapa ③
+351 21 404 4848

Cristal, a small pastry shop in the posh residential district of Lapa, has truly mouth-watering *pastéis*. The shop has more than once been awarded with the title of 'the best pastel de nata in the city'. (The Pastéis de Belém never enter this competition because they claim to be a category on their own.)

83 **MANTEIGARIA**
Rua do Loreto 2
Chiado ⑥
+351 21 347 1492

One of the latest additions to the *pastel de nata* scene in Lisbon, Manteigaria is a modern shop that wants to set a new standard of quality and design in the market. The tarts are baked the whole day long so you'll be sure to get a warm one (or ones).

84 **NATA LISBOA**
Rua de Santa Cruz
do Castelo 7
Castelo ⑦
+351 21 887 2050
www.natalisboa.com

NATA Lisboa is a franchising concept, present in several locations in Lisbon and also abroad. The recipe was fine-tuned by pastry masters to ensure that the taste of the tarts would be exactly the same in Lisbon, London, Hong Kong or anywhere else in the world.

85 **ALOMA**
Rua Francisco
Metrass 67
Campo de Ourique ③
+351 21 396 3797
www.omelhorpastel
denatadelisboa.com

Aloma started as a small pastry shop in the neighbourhood of Campo de Ourique but after the success of their *pastel de nata* (they also were the winner of the city's best of the best title several times) they started opening more branches around town, namely in Mercado da Ribeira and in Chiado.

85 ALOMA

83 MANTEIGARIA

The 5 best places for
CODFISH

---

86 CASA DO BACALHAU
Rua do Grilo 54
Beato ⑨
+351 21 862 0000
www.acasa
dobacalhau.com

As the name indicates, the highlight at Casa do Bacalhau ('House of Codfish') is of course *bacalhau*. Occupying the vaulted brick ground floor of an 18th-century palace, the restaurant offers a themed codfish experience in over 25 different recipes, some traditional, others more contemporary.

87 CASA PORTUGUESA DO PASTEL DE BACALHAU
Rua Augusta 106-108
Baixa ⑥
+351 916 486 888
www.pastei
debacalhau.com

This little shop in Baixa has been the talk of the town since it opened and started selling codfish cakes with buttery Serra cheese inside, a combination that nobody had ever thought of and one that has gained crowds of followers and detractors alike.

88 GAMBRINUS

**Rua das Portas de
Santo Antão 23
Baixa ⑥
+351 21 342 1466
*www.gambrinus
lisboa.com***

Gambrinus opened its doors in 1936 and it has been a power restaurant ever since, attracting a steady stream of celebrities that love it for its traditional cuisine, prepared and served in a classical way that is very rare to experience in today's world. The gastronomic highlights include several codfish dishes.

89 SOLAR DOS PRESUNTOS

**Rua das Portas de
Santo Antão 150
Av. da Liberdade ④
+351 21 342 4253
*www.solar
dospresuntos.com***

The Cardoso family is at the helm of this temple of traditional Portuguese cuisine that holds a unique position in the Lisbon food scene. If offers a dazzling menu of fish and some of the best codfish dishes in town. Passers-by are attracted by the window with eye-catching *presuntos* (smoked hams) and a lobster tank.

90 SOLAR DOS NUNES

**Rua dos
Lusiadas 68-72
Alcântara ①
+351 21 364 7359
*www.solar
dosnunes.com***

Solar means 'manor house' in Portuguese, and the term is without a doubt used adequately in the name of this landmark restaurant run by the Nunes family. It's located in the residential district of Alcântara, right under the 25th of April bridge. Try the codfish Cataplana (cooked in traditional copper steamers).

The 5 best places for a
ROMANTIC DINNER

---

91 **À PARTE**
Avenida Defensores
de Chaves 14-C
Saldanha ⑧
+351 21 354 3068
www.a-parte.com

À Parte occupies a ground-floor apartment of a residential building in Saldanha. The restaurant is spread over the rooms of the apartment, which have kept their original character, so it feels like several restaurants in one. There are also two terraces perfect for dining alfresco in warmer months.

92 **TAGUS BY SUSHIC**
Quinta do Tagus
Montinhoso,
Costas de Cão,
Monte da Caparica
Almada ①
+351 21 191 1965
www.sushic.pt

Sushic is a sushi restaurant on the south bank of the Tagus river that has received plenty of praise since it opened. The restaurant is located on an estate overlooking the river and the view is quite breathtaking. To add to it you can hire a helicopter to cross the river and arrive at the restaurant. Pretty chic, no?

93 **ATIRA-TE AO RIO**
Cais do Ginjal 69
Almada ①
+351 21 275 1380
www.atirateaorio.pt

You can reach Atira-te ao Rio (which translates to 'Throw yourself in the river') by car, crossing the bridge, or by taking the ferry to Cacilhas and then walking a few minutes on a boardwalk that lines the river and offers amazing views of the city. It's a gem of a place.

94 CAFÉ DE SÃO BENTO

Rua de São Bento 212
Príncipe Real ⑤
+351 21 395 2911
www.cafesaobento.com

Located next to the Parliament, Café de São Bento is a small and intimate bar that claims to serve the best steak in Lisbon. Don't expect a long list of options, people go there for the meat, the french fries and the mashed spinaches, and that's it. But it is well worth it.

95 CHAPITÔ À MESA

Costa do Castelo 7
Castelo ⑦
+351 21 887 5077
www.chapito.org

It's hard to beat the view this restaurant offers, located below the castle walls in the quarter of Castelo. Next to the amazing scenery and the menu, Restô has even more selling points, as it is part of Chapitô, an acclaimed cultural institution in Lisbon that includes a circus school, a theatre and an arts-and-crafts centre. A must-see.

The 5 best restaurants for
MEAT

---

96 OFÍCIO

Rua Nova da Trindade 10 Chiado ⑥
+351 91 045 6440
oficio-restaurant. negocio.site

Ofício was a hit from the outset because of its well-connected owners and the originality of its concept. The restaurant serves meat on the bone only, based on the idea (both interesting and true) that these are the most succulent cuts. Try the Godzilla-like *Chambão* and you'll immediately understand why people love this place so much.

97 RUBRO

Rua Rodrigues Sampaio 35 Av. da Liberdade ④
+351 21 314 4656
www.restaurante rubro.com

Rubro serves outstanding aged meats and has all the knowledge about how to prepare them. The Chuletón and the Cordero Lechal are to die for. The restaurant has two locations, one off Av. da Liberdade, the other in the bullfighting ring. Great wine selection.

98 SALA DE CORTE

Praça Dom Luís I 7 Cais do Sodré ⑥
+351 21 346 0030
www.saladecorte.pt

Sala de Corte is one of the city's favourite meat restaurants because of the quality of the meat (aged in the restaurant and cooked while you look on), the striking setting and the superb service. The restaurant has a lovely outdoor patio.

99 CAFÉ BUENOS AIRES

**Calçada do
Duque 31-B
Chiado** ⑥
+351 21 342 0739
*www.cafe
buenosaires.pt*

This small restaurant is a favourite among the younger travellers that flock into Lisbon. It is intimate, warm and relaxed, and on the menu there are mostly Argentinean dishes, including succulent meats. They have a sister restaurant, Fábrica, located less than a block away and also very fun to go to.

100 VICENTE

**Rua das Flores, 6
Cais do Sodré** ⑥
+351 21 21 806 6142

Vicente is the 'son' of the Carpinteiro Albino family, who have been raising cattle in the Alentejo region for generations. All the meat served here comes from this rural area. The restaurant occupies a former coal warehouse (a great fit for a restaurant that grills meat, no?) that still has its original brick-domed interior.

The 5 best restaurants for
PETISCOS

---

101 TAPAS 52

Rua Dom Pedro V 52
Príncipe Real ⑤
+351 21 343 2389

This small Spanish tapas restaurant is one of the busiest in town. The atmosphere is cheerful, the service is fast and friendly and the location is great. The tall tables outside are perfect for having a drink and a bite while watching people pass by on their way to and from Chiado.

102 ESPUMANTARIA DO PETISCO

Calçada do Marquês
de Tancos 1
Castelo ⑦
+351 96 551 5200

This small and intimate restaurant at the foot of the Castle offers a menu of *petiscos* (Portuguese tapas) and a wide selection of wines, sparkling wines and champagne. The outdoor terrace overlooks the roofs of the city and is a very pleasant place to linger during the day and to enjoy warmer nights.

103 CHIRINGUITO TAPAS BAR

R. Correia Teles 31-B
Campo de Ourique ③
+351 21 131 4432

This restaurant serves the best tapas in town, by far. The quality of the ingredients is outstanding and they are prepared with great care by the owners themselves, members of a traditional Portuguese family. The décor resembles that of a countryside manor house.

104 PETISCOS NO BAIRRO

Rua da Atalaia 133
Bairro Alto ⑥
+351 91 957 4498

This charming little tavern tucked away in Bairro Alto offers a savoury menu with a wide selection of well-priced and authentic *petiscos* and also some house specialties like the bean rice stew or the swordfish filet with Madeira wine sauce.

105 TABERNA TOSCA

Praça de São Paulo 21
Cais do Sodré ⑥
+351 21 803 4563
www.tabernatosca.com

Taberna Tosca was one of the first restaurants to open in Cais do Sodré after this formerly shabby part of the city started becoming the hippest place to be, especially for a night out. The restaurant is set in an 18th-century building and it offers a terrace across the street for alfresco dining.

À MARGEM

65 PLACES TO GO FOR A DRINK AND PARTY

The 5 best bars to
DRINK LIKE A LOCAL

---

106 PUB LISBOETA
Rua Dom Pedro V 63
Príncipe Real ⑤

Small is beautiful and so is Pub Lisboeta. Locals flock to this tiny bar in Príncipe Real to have a drink and to socialise. It's a great place for an aperitif. They serve a menu of imaginative bite-sized snacks and homemade pizzas.

107 CASA INDEPENDENTE
Largo do Intendente
Pina Manique 45
Chiado ⑧
+351 21 887 5143

Casa Independente is one of those places that are proof of Lisbon's diversity. The bar is located on the first floor of an extravagant building on the Intendente square, formerly a no-go zone because of the illegal activities that went on around there.

108 BICAENSE CAFÉ
Rua da Bica de
Duarte Belo 38-42
Santa Catarina ⑤
+351 21 325 7940
www.facebook.com/
bicaensereloaded

Bicaense is a Lisbon icon and has brought a taste of nightlife to the very traditional and authentic Bica neighbourhood, where the funicular runs along a steep slope lined with locals' homes, small shops and restaurants. Famous for its easy-going atmosphere and its cultural programming (live music, DJ's, movie screenings), this is a true gem in the city.

109 SANTOS

Santos ③

Santos is a vibrant nightlife quarter, especially popular with local youngsters, who meet up in the bars and cafes of this area before going out to party in the nearby discos of Avenida 24 de Julho, Docas, or Cais do Sodré. On weekend nights the sidewalks are full of people having fun.

110 TOPO

**Centro Comercial
Martim Moniz,
6th Floor
Baixa ③
+351 21 588 1322
*www.topo-lisboa.pt***

Topo is the brainchild of a group of local entrepreneur friends who decided to renovate the abandoned top floor of a decaying shopping centre on the up-and-coming square of Martim Moniz. They created a venue where hip locals gather for a drink and a bite, while enjoying the amazing view of the old city and the castle. A sister venue has opened in Chiado.

5 of the
COOLEST BARS

---

111 PENSÃO AMOR
Rua do Alecrim 19
Cais do Sodré ⑥
+351 21 314 3399
www.pensaoamor.pt

The story of this cool bar goes back to the time when the area of Cais do Sodré was the city's red light district. The bar, packed every night of the week, is located in a former inn that rented rooms by the hour to the local prostitutes. The décor is burlesque and there is even a pole for clients who want to have fun poledancing.

112 O BOM O MAU E O VILÃO
Rua do Alecrim 21
Cais do Sodré ⑥
+351 96 453 1423

O Bom, o Mau e o Vilão (which means 'the good, the bad and the vilain') is a cocktail bar in the hip area of Cais do Sodré. The bar, a reconverted 18th-century apartment, has several rooms and hosts weekly live music gigs by local bands. There are several resident DJs.

113 BAR 49 DA ZDB

Rua da Barroca 49
Bairro Alto ⑤
+351 21 343 0205
www.zedosbois.org

This cultural space in the heart of Bairro Alto is in fact a non-profit organisation that programs musical, theater and art happenings. The bar (with a secluded roof terrace for warm nights) is only open to members but not to worry, you can become a visiting member in an instant and then go straight to the bar. It's open on Fridays and Saturdays only and it is a very well kept secret, even for locals.

114 THE GEORGE

Rua do Crucifixo 58
Baixa ⑥
+351 21 346 0596
www.thegeorge
lisbon.com

Inspired by the English gastropubs, The George is a fun bar in the Baixa area that attracts people who want to watch sports broadcasts on the large TV screens and to enjoy their wide selection of beers and gins, and also to taste typical British favourites like Yorkshire pudding or the Sunday roast.

115 DUPLEX

Rua Nova do
Carvalho 58-60
Cais do Sodré ⑥
+351 91 516 2808
www.duplexrb.pt

Duplex, as the name implies, is divided into two spaces: a ground-floor bar that also serves tapas, and a first-floor restaurant where Chef Nuno Bergonse offers a comfort food menu in a casual yet sophisticatcd dimly-lit atmosphere. Look for the striking piece of art by local artist Bordalo II.

The 5 best
WINE BARS

---

116 CHAFARIZ DO VINHO
Praça da Algeria
Av. da Liberdade ④
+351 21 342 2079
www.chafarizdo
vinho.com

Owned by one of Portugal's leading wine journalists, João Paulo Martins, this wine bar is truly phenomenal. Not only because of the quality of the wine and the tapas selection, but also because of the stunning location inside an old water cistern that supplied the neighbourhood with fresh water.

117 GARRAFEIRA ALFAIA
Rua do Diário de
Notícias 125
Bairro Alto ⑥
+351 21 343 3079
www.garrafeiraalfaia.
com/wine

Located in the heart of Bairro Alto, Alfaia is a great place to discover the variety and quality of Portuguese wines while tasting some delicious tapas. It is famous for the friendliness of owner Pedro Marques (affectionately called 'Pedrão'), who is always present to suggest a surprising wine.

118 SOMMELIER
Rua do Telhal 59
Av. da Liberdade ④
+351 96 624 4446
www.sommelier.pt

Located on a side street of Avenida da Liberdade, Sommelier is a restaurant that combines fine dining dishes with the tasting of more than 80 fine wines by the glass, carefully selected by the restaurant's expert sommeliers.

119 BY THE WINE

Rua das Flores 41-43
Chiado ⑥
+351 21 342 0319

Large-scale wine producer José Maria da Fonseca (JMF), a company that has been making wines for almost 200 years, created this bar. Here you can enjoy JMF's wines, namely the world-famous Setúbal muscatels. The bar looks like a wine cellar and the arched ceilings are covered with a stunning display of 3200 bottles.

120 VESTIGIUS

Rua da Cintura do
Porto de Lisboa,
Arm. A 17
Cais do Sodré ⑥
+351 21 820 3320
www.vestigius.pt

This bar is worth a visit if only for the location on the riverside near Cais do Sodré. During the day you can enjoy the outdoor terrace overlooking the river and choose from a large selection of wines and cocktails. If you feel like it, go next door to Station, one of the coolest clubs in town.

119 **BY THE WINE**

The 5 best places for
SITTING IN THE SUN

---

121 À MARGEM

**Doca do Bom
Sucesso
Belém** ②
+351 91 862 0032
www.amargem.com

The minimalistic À Margem has no need for a fancy décor to compete with the sight of the wide river right in front. The location is in fact superb, two steps away from the Tagus, on the river boardwalk that links two of the city's most striking monuments: the Padrão dos Descobrimentos and the Belém Tower.

122 ZAMBEZE

**Mercado do Chão
do Loureiro
Mouraria** ⑦
+351 21 887 7056
*www.zambeze
restaurante.pt*

Zambeze is a peculiar restaurant that blends the cuisine from Mozambique with that from a region of Central Portugal, Beira. Its outdoor terrace, on the other hand, is all about Lisbon alone. The view on the river and the hill of Chiado is mind-blowing, with the castle and the Sé church as a backdrop.

125 **ESPELHO D'ÁGUA**

123 PORTAS DO SOL

Largo das Portas do Sol
Alfama ⑦
+351 21 885 1299
www.portasdosol.biz

This terrace overlooks the whole of Alfama, Lisbon's most picturesque quarter, a millenary maze of narrow streets and alleys that extends from the Castle down to the river. The view is difficult to rival, even in a city with so many breathtaking viewpoints. Everyone will love the myriad of brick-coloured rooftops.

124 RIBEIRA DAS NAUS – QUIOSQUE

Avenida Ribeira das Naus 5
Cais do Sodré ⑥
+351 91 742 7013

This kiosk was opened when the waterfront promenade of Ribeira das Naus was renovated. It was here that the Portuguese built the ships that cruised the seas to Asia, Africa and the Americas. The outdoor terrace offers a breathtaking view of the Tagus and the 25th of April bridge.

125 ESPELHO D'ÁGUA

Avenida de Brasilia
Edifício Espelho d'Água
Belém ②
+351 21 301 0510
www.espacoespelho deagua.com

Built in the 40s as part of the Exhibition of the Portuguese World, this pavilion has lived many lives since. Today it has been fully renovated according to the original design and has regained all its glory. The terrace opens to the Padrão dos Descobrimentos, one of Lisbon's top landmarks.

The 5 best
COCKTAIL BARS

---

126 CINCO LOUNGE
Rua Ruben A. Leitão
Príncipe Real ⑤
+351 21 342 4033
www.cincolounge.com

Dave Palenthorne came from the UK to Lisbon a few years ago and set out to revolutionise the city's cocktail scene, which was very dull at the time of his arrival. His Cinco Lounge is still in the forefront of the local cocktail culture, and it is a true temple for connoisseurs and aficionados.

127 RED FROG
Rua do Salitre 5A
Av. da Liberdade ④
+351 21 583 1120

This cocktail bar was based on the American speakeasies of the 1920s and, to add to the theme, there even is a secret room that can be accessed by pushing a wall. The cocktail list has been made up by London Nightjar's Marian Beke, who is responsible for the English bar's presence on the list of the best bars in the world.

128 GIN LOVERS

128 GIN LOVERS

**Praça do Príncipe
Real 26
Príncipe Real ⑤
+351 21 347 1341
www.ginlovers.pt**

Gin Lovers is a well-rounded concept that encompasses the world's first magazine dedicated to gin, a highly informative website, a couple of shops, a line of merchandising (kits to prepare drinks at home, etc.), and this bar located inside the Embaixada Concept Store in Príncipe Real.

129 DOUBLE9

**Rua da
Misericórdia 76
Chiado ⑥
+351 21 248 1480
www.mercyhotel.com**

The cool 9Hotel Mercy in Chiado houses this Tea Cocktail Bar that offers two different concepts: a modern tearoom during the day and a cocktail bar at night. All cocktails blend alcohol and tea, giving the drinks a new layer of tastes and aromas that is sure to entice the senses.

130 MATIZ POMBALINA

**Rua das Trinas 25
Lapa ③
+351 21 404 3703
www.matiz-
pombalina.pt**

This bar is located in the posh residential area of Lapa and occupies the ground floor of an 18th-century building. It is true to the feel of days gone by, with old tile panels and baroque-style furnishings throughout its rooms. The sound of blues, soul, bossa nova and jazz plays softly in the background.

The 5 best places to have a good
CUP OF COFFEE

———

131 CLAUDIO CORALLO
Rua da Escola
Politécnica 4
Príncipe Real ⑤
+351 21 386 2158
www.claudio
corallo.com

Regarded as one of the top chocolatiers in the world, Italian-born Claudio Corallo offers a fully integrated chocolate and coffee concept, from his organic cocoa and coffee plantation on the African island of São Tomé (a former Portuguese colony) to this hip shop in Príncipe Real's busiest street.

132 TARTINE
Rua Serpa Pinto 15-A
Chiado ⑥
+351 21 342 9108
www.tartine.pt

Located on a quiet street in Chiado, just off the busy Rua Garret, this French inspired bakery/cafe offers homemade breads and traditional Portuguese pastries like the famous custard tarts. If you want to go crazy on the calories ask for Tartine's signature treat, the Chiado cake.

133 KAFFEEHAUS

Rua Anchieta 3
Chiado ⑥
+351 21 095 6828
www.kaffeehaus-
lisboa.com

This Viennese-inspired coffee house was opened by two Austrian friends and immediately became one of the city's top addresses for coffee, light meals and Sunday brunch. The menu includes Austrian specialties like *Wiener Schnitzel*, *Sacher-Torte*, *Apfelstrudel* and mulled wine, plus daily specials shown on a chalkboard.

134 CAFÉ ROYALE

Largo Rafael Bordalo
Pinheiro 29
Chiado ⑥
+351 21 346 9125
www.royalecafe.com

Another Chiado favourite, the Café Royale, is an enchanting place to go for a drink or a light meal. The cafe has three different atmospheres, perfect for all weather conditions and times of day: the outdoor terrace on the square, the stylish and warm interior and a secluded courtyard with a vertical garden.

135 COPENHAGEN COFFEE LAB CAFÉ

Rua Nova da
Piedade 10
Príncipe Real ⑤
+351 91 660 4054
www.cphcoffeelab.pt

This Danish-style coffee shop is a stone's throw away from Praça das Flores, one of Lisbon's coolest little squares. The Danish owners wanted to make this more than just a cafe and created a coffee experience shop where clients can enjoy several kinds of coffees, each prepared or served differently.

The 5 most
BEAUTIFUL CAFES

---

136 CAFÉ A BRASILEIRA
Rua Garrett 120
Chiado ⑥
+351 21 346 9541

Brasileira is Lisbon's most iconic cafe. Opened in 1905 (when it only sold coffee from Brazil, hence the name), it is a tourist destination in itself, not only for its dazzling Art Deco interiors but also for the bronze statue of poet Fernando Pessoa sitting on a table on the cafe's outdoor terrace.

137 CAFÉ NICOLA
Praça Dom
Pedro IV 24-25
Baixa ⑥
+351 21 346 0579

The Nicola cafe is said to date from the 1700s, when an Italian called Nicola opened it on Rossio square. It soon became popular with artists and personalities of those days – namely the famous poet Bocage, for instance, was a regular patron. The décor dates from 1929, which explains the Art Deco motifs.

138 PASTELARIA VERSAILLES

Avenida da República 15-A
Saldanha ⑧
+351 21 354 6340

Versailles has been an institution in Lisbon since it opened its doors in 1922 on the then recently built Avenida da República, one of the city's so-called 'New Avenues'. Its patisserie is famous in the city for its variety and quality. There is also a restaurant serving Portuguese food, which is very popular for lunch during the week.

139 LEITARIA A CAMPONEZA

Rua dos Sapateiros 155
Baixa ⑥
+351 92 313 2488

Although this pretty small *leitaria* (milk shop) was just a cafe for many years, it now also operates as a restaurant. It opened its doors in 1907 and still has the original décor, including the valuable *azulejos* (a unique sort of ceramic tiles). People go there for the surprising Art Nouveau interiors and the vintage façade. There's a small terrace outside.

140 PASTELARIA SÃO ROQUE

Rua Dom Pedro V 57
Príncipe Real ⑤
+351 21 322 4350
www.panifsroque.pt

Founded in the early 20th century, Pastelaria São Roque is one of the finest examples of Art Nouveau architecture in Lisbon. The interior is not what you would expect in a cafe, with a large domed ceiling sustained by marble columns and decorated with gilded motifs.

The 5 nicest places for
GAYS *and* LESBIANS

---

141 TRUMPS

**Rua da Imprensa
Nacional 104
Príncipe Real ⑤
+351 91 593 8266
*www.trumps.pt***

This is one of the first gay clubs in
Lisbon, dating from the 80s, and it holds
a unique position in the city, not just
in the gay community. These days the
club is straight-friendly and on a normal
night the crowd will be diverse and
eclectic, with gay men, gay women and
straight people.

142 FINALMENTE

**Rua da Palmeira 38
Príncipe Real ⑤
+351 21 347 9923
*www.finalmente
club.com***

Finalmente is a classic gay club that has
been open since 1976 in the quarter
of Príncipe Real, Lisbon's 'gaybourhood'.
It is well-known for its drag queen
performances, especially those of the
resident drag queen stars Deborah
Krystall and Samantha Rox. The music
is mostly house.

143 GAYOLA

**Rua da Imprensa
Nacional 116-B
Príncipe Real ⑤
+351 21 397 4493**

Gayola (*gaiola* in Portuguese means
'bird cage') is a bar and steakhouse open
to both gay and straight patrons. The
atmosphere is relaxing and easygoing
and it is one of the few places in town
where you can eat until late at night,
namely 3 am.

144 PUREX

**Rua das
Salgadeiras 28
Bairro Alto ⑥
+351 21 342 8061**

Purex is a gay-friendly bar in Bairro Alto, a quarter that historically has always been one of the gay haunts in Lisbon. There is no sign outside but the bright orange door is hard to miss. Inside, the dark ambiance and the well-selected music invite clients to the small dance floor, which gets packed later in the night.

145 WOOFLX

**Rua da Palmeira 44-B
Príncipe Real ⑤
+351 21 346 8418**

This bar started off as a meeting place for the 'bears' community in Lisbon (gays with a strong masculine look) but now attracts all gay crowds. The owners have another gay bar nearby, WoofX, a harder core version of WoofLx, where clients, 'bears' and others, go to play out their fetishes.

The 5 best places for
FADO

---

146 MESA DE FRADES
**Rua dos
Remédios 139-A
Alfama ⑦
+351 91 702 9436**

There is no fado restaurant in town that can rival the beauty of Mesa de Frades. Located in an 18th-century former chapel where the walls and floors are covered with authentic glazed tiles, the intimate room only seats a handful, so be sure to book beforehand. The candle-lit atmosphere is warm and inviting.

147 CLUBE DE FADO
**Rua de São João
da Praça 86-94
Alfama ⑦
+351 21 885 2704
*www.clube-de-
fado.com***

Here is an upscale version of a fado restaurant, and everything plays into that, from the décor to the service, from the food to the type of fado that is sung. In fact you will listen to an aristocratic version of fado, as opposed to the street fado (*vadio*) that is brought to you at most fado places.

148 A BAIUCA

Rua de São Miguel 20
Alfama ⑦
+351 21 342 1386

Family-owned and -operated A Baiuca is a place where you can expect genuine fado performances, with people from the neighbourhood coming over to sing *fado vadio* (vagrant fado). Even the cooks are known to stop their kitchen tasks from time to time to start singing, much to the surprise of patrons.

149 TASCA DO CHICO

Rua do Diário de
Notícias 39
Bairro Alto ⑥
+351 96 505 9670

This small and intimate bar/eatery (with locations in Bairro Alto and Alfama) is a place to enjoy fado music in an informal and convivial setting. The warm and dimly-lit ambiance is conducive to experiencing the heartfelt tunes, brought by singers that go around in and out different fado restaurants.

150 SENHOR VINHO

Rua do Meio
à Lapa 18
Lapa ③
+351 21 397 2681
www.srvinho.com

Senhor Vinho owes its high standing to its charismatic owner, the famous fado singer Maria da Fé, who still sings there regularly, adding a touch of stardom to the experience. It is by far the classiest fado restaurant in the city, and the quality of the food matches the well-appointed décor and the personalised service.

The 5 best places to
DANCE

---

151 LUX

**Avenida Infante
Dom Henrique
Santa Apolónia** ⑨
+351 21 882 0890
www.luxfragil.com

LUX is the only club in Lisbon that deserves a spot on the list of the best dancing clubs in the world. Owner Manuel Reis installed it in a former warehouse by the river; there are two floors plus a rooftop terrace for the warmer months.

152 MUSICBOX

**Rua Nova do
Carvalho 24
Cais do Sodré** ⑥
+351 21 347 3188
*www.musicbox
lisboa.com*

Opened in 2006 in a nice spot in the shabby-chic area of Cais do Sodré, Musicbox is part performing stage, part dance floor. It is housed in a ground-floor vaulted room that dates from the late 1800s, which naturally increases the quality of the sound experience, and is also part of the reason for its success.

153 SILK

**Rua da
Misericórdia 14
Chiado** ⑥
+351 91 300 9193
www.silk-club.com

Silk is Lisbon's most exclusive nightclub and often you will need to be on the guest list to get in – so call beforehand to reserve a spot, especially on weekend nights. The club is located on the top floor of an office building in Chiado and offers a strikingly beautiful panorama of historic Lisbon and the river.

154 RIVE-ROUGE

Mercado da Ribeira
Cais do Sodré ⑥
+351 21 346 1117
www.rive-rouge.com

Owned by the local nightlife guru Manuel Reis, Rive-Rouge is decorated in red *(rouge)* and sits on the north bank *(rive)* of the Tagus, hence its name. The red comes from the fact that this area was the city's red light district, before becoming hip and trendy. It's open from the early evening onwards for after-work drinks till late at night for dancing.

155 B.LEZA

Cais Gás 1
Cais do Sodré ⑥
+351 21 010 6837

A one-of-a-kind African club opened in 1995. For almost 20 years it has been doing a commendable job of promoting African music (especially music hailing from Cape Verde) and culture, and it draws a legion of fans that come to dance to the beat of the Black Continent.

The 5 nicest
ROOFTOP AND OTHER TERRACES

---

156 RIO MARAVILHA

**LX Factory,
Entrada 3, Piso 4
Rua Rodrigues
Faria 103
Alcântara ①
+351 96 602 8229
*www.riomaravilha.pt***

Here's one of the coolest restaurants and bars in town. Located on the top floor of one of the dilapidated buildings of LX Factory, the restaurant offers stunning views of the river and the statue of Christ the King, which was inspired by the Christ the Redeemer statue of Rio de Janeiro. The outdoor rooftop bar is as hip as bars can be.

157 HOTEL DO CHIADO

**Rua Nova do
Almada 114
Chiado ⑥
+351 21 325 6100
*www.hoteldochiado.pt***

Located at the Hotel do Chiado, this terrace offers an impressive view over the Castle and the Baixa quarters, with the omnipresent river lining the picture on the right-hand side. The cosy interior room with oversized windows is filled with inviting sofas and has an oyster bar.

158 DARWIN CAFÉ

**Avenida Brasília
Ala B
Belém ②
+351 21 048 0222
*www.darwincafe.com***

Upon his death, Portuguese mogul António Champalimaud donated a large portion of his wealth to set up a Foundation to foster medical research in the field of eyesight. Located at the foundation's 'Center for the Unknown', near the mouth of the Tagus, the Darwin Café is probably the most impressive riverside terrace in town.

159 LE CHAT

Jardim 9 de Abril
Santos ③
+351 21 396 3668

A truly magnificent terrace cafe located on the edge of a secluded garden next to the Antique Art Museum. The contemporary architecture of the cafe, designed as a glass structure, blends perfectly with the garden and the openness of the river that lies at its feet.

160 INSÓLITO

Rua São Pedro de
Alcântara 83
Chiado ©
+351 21 130 3306
www.theinsolito.pt

Owned by the D'Eça Leal brothers, who also own the adjacent The Decadent, Insólito is true to its Portuguese name, which means 'unusual'. It's located on the top floor of a palace that overlooks the viewpoint of São Pedro de Alcântara and offers a mind-blowing view over the old city, the castle and the river.

160 INSÓLITO

The 5 best
BARS FROM ANOTHER TIME

---

161 PROCÓPIO
Alto de São Francisco 21-A Amoreiras ④ +351 21 385 2851 *www.barprocopio.com*

Everything at Procópio appears to be from a long lost time, starting with the entrance, in a seemingly rural alleyway off the Amoreiras garden. Once you ring the doorbell and go in, you will feel like a time traveler who just went 100 years back into the past, to an Art-Nouveau-style bohemian cafe in Paris, frequented by intellectuals.

162 PAVILHÃO CHINÊS
Rua Dom Pedro V 89 Príncipe Real ⑤ +351 21 342 4729

This surely is one of the most beautiful bars in the world. Well, calling it a bar falls short of what Pavilhão Chinês really is. It would be fairer to call it a museum of toys and curiosities, given the dazzling collection that's on display in every square centimetre of the five labyrinth-like rooms.

163 FOXTROT

Tv. Santa Teresa 28
Príncipe Real ⑤
+351 21 395 2697
www.barfoxtrot.pt

A gem of a bar located in a quiet street of the Príncipe Real quarter. The vibe is a blend of the classical Lisbon bar atmosphere with that of an English pub. As you could expect (and hope for) there is a fireplace and a pool table. You can also enjoy some food until late in the night.

164 RESISTÊNCIA LISBOA

Calçada do Marquês
de Abrantes 82
Santos ③
+351 91 883 8317

This new place in Santos, which is managed by the owners of La Boulangerie, has much more to offer than most bars. It was created to bring together lovers of music, cinema, literature and board games in a place where they can enjoy culture while sipping cocktails and nibbling on traditional Portuguese *petiscos*.

165 SNOB BAR

Rua do Século 178
Príncipe Real ⑤
+351 21 346 3723
www.snob
arestaurante.com

Open since the 70s, this secluded bar has since then been a favourite hangout for journalists, artists and politicians, who love the quiet atmosphere and the famous steak. You will need to ring the bell to be allowed in by the owner himself, who makes a point of welcoming every guest at the door.

The 5 best
LISBON AREA WINES

---

166 MOSCATEL DE SETÚBAL

Moscatel is a very aromatic grape variety that has hints of citrus and flowery flavours. It ripens to high sugar levels and is ideal for making sweet wines. The Moscatel wines from the Peninsula of Setúbal (30 minutes south of Lisbon) have been produced for over 200 years and have achieved world fame.

167 QUINTA DO MONTE D'OIRO

Award-winning estate Quinta do Monte d'Oiro, located in Alenquer, 40 miles north of Lisbon, was founded by winemaker José Bento dos Santo in 1990. He set out to make top-quality, deep, mineral and personalised wines that respect his vineyard's unique terroir.

168 COLARES AND CARCAVELOS WINES

Nowadays very little wine is still produced in the famous wine regions of Colares and Carcavelos, located west of Lisbon. In Carcavelos tiny quantities of fortified sweet wine are produced, from red or white local grapes. In Colares high-acid, tannic red wines are made, as well as gently aromatic whites based on Malvasia.

169 LISBON DOC WINES

Lisboa is a wine region with nine sub-regions that stretches along the Atlantic coastline and is characterised by small undulating hills and a temperate climate. The traditional white varieties of wine produced here include Arinto, Fernão Pires and Malvasia, and for reds you should try Alicante Bouschet, Aragonez and Castelão.

170 JOSÉ MARIA DA FONSECA

José Maria da Fonseca is a two-century-old wine family business, the oldest in the Setúbal region. The nearly 650 hectares of vineyards produce high-quality wines, such as Periquita, Domini, José de Sousa and Alambre. The company has a very good visitors' centre in Azeitão.

LUVARIA ULLICES

70 PLACES
TO SHOP

The 5 most inspiring
FASHION
DESIGNERS

171 ALVES/GONÇALVES

Travessa Guillherme
Cossoul 16
Chiado ⑥
+351 21 346 3125

Celebrity fashion designer duo Manuel Alves and José Manuel Gonçalves have a concept shop in Chiado where they show their haute couture and prêt-à-porter creations but where clients can also experience salon services (hair, body, make-up) in a sophisticated setting.

172 NUNO GAMA

Rua de O Século 171
Príncipe Real ⑤
+351 21 347 9068

One of the leading fashion designers in Portugal is Nuno Gama, whose menswear collections are inspired by Portuguese culture and the country's iconography. At his Príncipe Real concept store he sells clothing, footware and accessories, and there is also a hip barbershop.

173 LIDIJA KOLOVRAT

Rua Dom Pedro V 79
Príncipe Real ⑤
+351 21 387 4536
www.lidijakolovrat.org

The boutique and atelier of Bosnia-born Lidija Kolovrat are in the heart of Príncipe Real, the quarter for cutting-edge designers in Lisbon. There she sells her collections and also accessories and a range of decorative items for the home.

174 DINO ALVES

Rua da Madalena 91,
1dto
Baixa ⑥
+351 21 886 5252
www.dinoalves.eu

Dino Alves does some of the most creative fashion work in Portugal, never shying away from using original and even provocative materials and styling features. His genius has made him a regular presence at the country's fashion shows and his brand is a synonym of risk-taking and an artistic approach to fashion.

175 FILIPE FAÍSCA

Calçada do
Combro 99
Chiado ⑤
+351 21 342 0014
www.filipefaisca.com

A well-known name in the Portuguese fashion scene, Filipe Faísca, started presenting his creations back in the 90s, venturing out into fashion fields like cinema and theatre wardrobe design and also making the most amazing shopping windows in town. His urban vintage style pieces are beautifully produced.

The 5 coolest
FASHION SHOPS

---

176 OFICINA MUSTRA

Rua Rodrigues
Sampaio 81
Av. da Liberdade ④
+351 21 314 7009

This well-guarded secret of a shop is located on a parallel street of Av. da Liberdade, tucked away in a walled garden that is easy to miss as you pass by. Veríssimo Mustra and his wife Fatima take a very unique approach to fashion, acting as personal stylists for clients that seek their Italian style men's clothes.

177 FASHION CLINIC

Avenida da
Liberdade 180
Av. da Liberdade ④
+351 21 354 9040
www.fashionclinic.pt

Paula Amorim, from the well-known and wealthy Amorim family, owns this fashion store on Av. da Liberdade (with a menswear shop further down the street) and also the Gucci store and a share in Tom Ford's global brand. It's easy to understand that this is the top address for luxury in town, offering a very well-chosen selection.

178 BUBBLES COMPANY

Amoreiras Shopping
Center
Amoreiras ④
+351 91 172 3013

This clothing store in the posh Amoreiras Shopping Center sells a very exclusive, well-priced and carefully selected multi-brand collection of women's wear, ranging from classic-contemporary to bohemian-chic.

179 AMÉLIE AU THEATRE

Rua da Escola
Politécnica 69-71
Príncipe Real ⑤
+351 21 598 2900
www.amelie-autheatre.com

This very special French-inspired boutique was created by Amélia Antunes (hence 'Amélie au theatre'), a local designer of fashion accessories. At her Príncipe Real shop Amélia sells a well-selected range of shoes, jewelry and fashion pieces from an array of contemporary Portuguese designers.

180 PARIS EM LISBOA

Rua Garrett 77
Chiado ⑥
+351 21 342 4329
www.parisemlisboa.pt

Opened with great poise in 1888 in the heart of Chiado, this three-floor shop was the official supplier of the Royal Family, bringing to Lisbon the finest selection of Parisian fashion and fabrics. These days the shop also sells home fabrics and perfumes. The shop itself is a gem of 19th-century architecture.

5 unique
VINTAGE SHOPS

---

181 LOJA DA ATALAIA

Av. Infante Dom
Henrique,
Cais da Pedra
Santa Apolónia ⑨
+351 21 882 2578
www.lojadatalaia.com

Manuel Reis, the man behind dance club LUX, is also the creator of Loja da Atalaia, located in between the club and his other co-owned venture, Bica do Sapato. At his shop Manuel presents a personal selection of prized vintage furniture from the 50s up to the 70s, as well as some art pieces from local contemporary designers.

182 MUITO MUITO

LX Factory
R. Rodrigues
Faria 103
Alcântara ①
www.muitomuito.pt

Muito Muito, located inside LX Factory, is a well-curated vintage shop that sells mostly curiosities and small furniture pieces. The concept and selection of the shop is fitting to the whole LX Factory mood, a bohemian and vintage city within the city. Luis Mangas, the owner, offers expert help to clients.

183 CANTINHO DO VINTAGE

Avenida Infante D.
Henrique, Arm. 2
Santa Apolónia ⑨
+351 91 200 7552

Lisbon's largest outlet of vintage furniture, located in a gigantic warehouse in the Beato area. It showcases a multitude of pieces from Portugal, Germany, England and Scandinavia. Here you'll find items in all price ranges, and great bargains compared to similar shops abroad.

184 A OUTRA FACE DA LUA

Rua da Assunção 22
Baixa ⑥
+351 21 886 3430
www.aoutraface
dalua.com

Located in a stunning post-1755-earthquake building, A outra face da lua sells women's vintage clothing in a hippie-chic setting. The quality of the items is superior to any other similar shop in the city, and prices are still very reasonable. The shop has a cute cafe with some pleasant outdoor tables.

185 VINTAGE DEPARTMENT

Rua da Escola
Politécnica 42
Príncipe Real ⑤
+351 91 177 8837
www.vintage-
department.com

This hip vintage furniture store is the brainchild of Emily Plaister Tome and Alma Mollemans. The British-Dutch couple first opened a shop in Aachen, Germany, and later decided to bring it to Lisbon. The shop occupies the ground floor of a palace in Príncipe Real and is filled with mid-century modern pieces by iconic as well as lesser-known designers. You'll also find stunning taxidermy here.

The 5 most
UNUSUAL SHOPS

---

186 LUVARIA ULISSES

Rua do Carmo 87A
Chiado ⑥
+351 21 342 0295
*www.luvaria
ulisses.com*

This 'hand haute couture' shop is probably one of the smallest shops in the world, able to welcome only one client at a time inside its delightful Art Deco interior. As a member of a dying breed of classic shops, it sells gloves and only gloves, custom-made for each client.

187 CAZA DAS VELLAS LORETO

Rua do Loreto 53/5
Chiado ⑥
+351 21 342 5387
*www.cazavellas
loreto.com.pt*

This amazing shop has been selling candles of all shapes, sizes, aromas and colours since its opening in 1789. The wood-panelled shop itself is a gem of commercial architecture. As you walk in, you will feel as if you were thrown back in time to a world gone by, where service is more personal and attentive than you have ever experienced.

188 VIDA PORTUGUESA

Rua Anchieta 11
Chiado ⑥
+351 21 346 5073
*www.avida
portuguesa.com*

In these stunning traditional Portuguese giftshops all items on sale are carefully selected by Catarina Portas, the master-mind behind this incredible concept, which has helped many traditional manufacturers to find a second breath for their products.

189 CHAPELARIA D'AQUINO

Rua do
Comércio 16-A
Baixa ⑥
+351 91 227 7783

This is one of the few shops from another time that are still around in Lisbon. Chapelaria d'Aquino is a headwear specialty store that has been one of the preferred purveyors of hats for generations and generations of fashionable *Lisboetas*.

190 CASA PEREIRA

Rua Garrett 38
Chiado ⑥
+351 21 342 6694

Casa Pereira has been a family business since the early 20th century, and still is the place to shop for high-quality coffee beans, teas and chocolates. As in the past, the shop still sources many of its products from suppliers in the former Portuguese colonies, namely coffee and chocolate from São Tomé and Brazil.

188 VIDA PORTUGUESA

5 of the best
BOOK SHOPS

---

191 LIVRARIA FÉRIN
Rua Nova do
Almada 70-74
Chiado ⑥
+351 21 342 4492
www.ferin.pt

Livraria Férin has been in the same family for several generations, which has made it possible to keep the concept and the service as it has been since the store opened back in the 1840s. It is said to be the second oldest book shop in Portugal, which means that there are certainly many rare finds to look for on the shelves.

192 FÁBRICA DO BRAÇO DE PRATA
Rua da Fábrica de
Material de Guerra 1
Beato ⑨
+351 96 551 8068
www.braco
deprata.com

Here you can find books, no question about that, but the shop also acts as a vibrant cultural centre for the alternative hipster crowd, offering art exhibits, live music performances, lectures and even a restaurant. All this happens in the unique setting of a former factory in eastern Lisbon – it's a truly special place.

193 LER DEVAGAR

LX Factory
R. Rodrigues
Faria 103
Alcântara ①
+351 21 325 9992
www.lerdevagar.om

This wandering bookshop tried out several locations in Lisbon until it settled a few years ago in the hipster-chic LX Factory project, occupying a former warehouse lined with bookshelves. It has a loyal crowd of followers, which explains its resilience in today's difficult times for booksellers.

194 PÓ DOS LIVROS

Avenida Duque de
Avila 58-A
Avenidas Novas ⑧
+351 21 795 9339
*livrariapodoslivros.
blogspot.com*

This independent neighbourhood bookshop is praised for its personal and expert service, and for the quality and relevance of its literary selection. The owners make a point of promoting lesser known authors and publishing houses, and they also sell used books.

195 LIVRARIA BERTRAND

Rua Garrett 73-75
Chiado ⑥
+351 21 347 6122
*www.bertrand.pt/
livrarias-bertrand*

This is the world's oldest bookshop in operation, opened by the French Bertrand brothers in 1732. It is no longer a family business, in fact it is now the flagship store of a chain of bookshops (and a publishing house), but despite that it still has its original charm. There's an interesting selection of international magazines.

The 5 best
STREET MARKETS

---

196 FEIRA DA LADRA
Campo de
Santa Clara
Graça ⑦

Every Saturday and Tuesday morning locals and visitors flock to the Campo de Santa Clara square (next to the National Pantheon) to hunt for bargains and curiosities at Lisbon's most entertaining flea market. There's something for every budget.

197 MERCADO BIOLÓGICO DO PRÍNCIPE REAL
Praça do
Príncipe Real
Príncipe Real ⑤

Lisbon's only organic farmers market is held every Saturday morning around the Príncipe Real garden, which makes it a great place to pass by while visiting that enchanting quarter of the city. The market vendors offer vegetables, fruits, olive oil, fresh herbs and other produce of superior quality and excellent value for money.

198 LX FACTORY SUNDAY MARKET
LX Factory
R. Rodrigues
Faria 103
Alcântara ①
+351 21 314 3399
www.lxfactory.com

LX Factory is a successful urban renewal project that occupies a group of large abandoned 19th-century warehouses and factories in the area of Alcântara, keeping their raw and romantic feel intact. It is now the home of creative companies, artists, a fantastic restaurant and nightlife destination and the place to be for cultural activities.

199 MERCADO DO JARDIM

Jardim da Estrela
Estrela ③
+351 91 413 8287

The garden of Estrela is home to a Crafts&Design fair on the first weekend of every month (except for January and August), when vendors take over the garden paths, selling their artefacts, and local families bring their children to enjoy the outdoors. In summer people take advantage of the opportunity to picnic on the grass.

200 AV. DA LIBERDADE MARKET

Av. da Liberdade ④

The wide cobblestoned sidewalks of Av. da Liberdade host a regular antiques market (every second weekend of the month plus the fourth Saturday and the preceding Thursday from May to October) that is much more upscale than that of Feira da Ladra. It's the fanciest of street fairs in Lisbon, befitting of its posh location.

196 FEIRA DA LADRA

5 *of the best*
FLOWER SHOPS

―――――――

201 MERCADO DA RIBEIRA

Avenida 24 de
Julho 50
Cais do Sodré ⑥

After a large-scale renovation many new stalls and kiosks were added to Lisbon's largest market, but the old traditional vendors stayed as well. Among those are still a few flower shops. They are not the place to go for fancy flower arrangements, but you will find a nice variety of fresh flowers here, at a very fair price.

202 FLOWER POWER

Calçada do Combro 2
Chiado ⑥
+351 21 342 2381
www.flower
power.com.pt

This original flower shop on the edge of Chiado and Bairro Alto is known for its creative and contemporary flower arrangements. There is also a delightful little cafe serving light meals. The outside tables are very popular and that's no surprise.

203 FLOR FLOR

Largo Vitorino
Damásio 3-C – Pav. 3
Santos ③
+351 21 397 3050
www.florflor.pt

Flor Flor is owned by the Piano brothers, who have been in the flower business in Portugal and Angola for over 20 years. Their sense of style is widely known and their client list is there to prove that. Their shop is located in an inner courtyard in Santos with a very Parisian feel – a perfect place for a shop like this.

204 DECOFLORÁLIA

Rua Castilho, 185-C
Parque Eduardo VII ④
+351 21 387 2454
www.decofloralia.pt

One of Lisbon's most traditional florists, open since 1976 and known for their floral arrangements for weddings and events – they're the preferred supplier of the leading caterers and hotels in the city. The staff (30 people!) is expert in creating stunning decorative effects using fresh and dry flowers.

205 REPÚBLICA DAS FLORES

Rua da
Misericórdia 31
Chiado ⑥
+351 21 342 5073
*www.republica
dasflores.pt*

This is the place to buy out-of-the-ordinary flower arrangements, but in addition to that this unique concept store also sells fragrances, linen, home décor pieces, candles, exotic fabrics, champagne and sweets. It is a cave of Ali Baba in the heart of Lisbon.

205 REPÚBLICA DAS FLORES

The 5 best
DESIGN SHOPS

206 LINHA DA VIZINHA
Av. Conselheiro
Fernando de
Sousa 27A
Amoreiras ④
+351 21 382 5350
*www.alinhada
vizinha.pt*

Lisbon's top design shop, offering an array of leading home, garden and office furniture and lighting brands such as Vitra, Capellini, Fritz Hansen, Edra and Flos. The shop is the spearhead of a company that does major furniture contracting for corporate clients.

207 POEIRA
Rua da Imprensa à
Estrela 21B
Estrela ③
+351 21 395 4229
www.poeiraonline.com

Jet-setter interior designer Mónica Penaguião owns this unconventional design shop located on the street of the prime minister's palace (with twin shops in Rio de Janeiro and São Paulo). Mónica herself handpicks the selection on offer, a blend of international brands and artisan pieces.

208 ESPAÇO B
Rua Dom Pedro V 120
Príncipe Real ⑤
+351 21 346 1210
www.espaco-b.com

Owned by the same people that run B Bazar and Arquitectónica, this concept store offers an eclectic and sophisticated selection of men's and women's fashion (from brands like Comme des Garçons), art and design books, watches, perfumes, music CDs and scented candles.

209 NORD

Av. Infante Dom
Henrique, Cais da
Pedra, loja 6
Santa Apolónia ⑨
+351 21 882 1045
www.lojanord.com

NORD is a design shop in one of a series of cool former warehouses in Santa Apolónia that now house some of Lisbon's hippest addresses. It's a small shop that exclusively sells pieces from Nordic designers such as Cecilie Manz, Finn Juhl, Monica Förster and Arne Jacobsen, the greatest name in Scandinavian design.

210 ROOF

Rua Nova do Almada 1
Baixa ⑥
+351 21 325 8847
www.roof.pt

ROOF is a sophisticated interior design shop and studio located just below Chiado. Their collection, carefully selected by a team of designers and architects, consists of pieces that range from lighting to home and office furniture, as well as decorative accessories.

207 POEIRA

The 5 best
FOOD MARKETS

---

211 MERCADO DA RIBEIRA

Avenida 24
de Julho 50
Cais do Sodré ⑥
+351 21 359 3100

After having spent many years in a lethargic state, Lisbon's largest food market, Mercado da Ribeira (built in 1892), was renovated by Time Out magazine. New food stalls and kiosks were added but also the traditional market vendors stayed. The market quickly became the city's new food hub and the second most popular tourist attraction.

212 MERCADO DE CAMPO DE OURIQUE

Rua Coelho da Rocha
Campo de Ourique ③
+351 21 132 3701
www.mercado
decampodeourique.pt

This cosy neighbourhood food market in Campo de Ourique was the first in town to be renovated, setting the example for other markets. The new additions include a dozen food stalls that blend in perfectly with the traditional vendors of fish, vegetables and fruits. It's one of the city's hotspots.

213 MERCADO DE ALVALADE NORTE

Avenida Rio de
Janeiro 27
Alvalade ⑧
+351 21 849 1860

Located in the north of Lisbon, in the neighbourhood it was named after, this food market is celebrated for the quality of its products. It has yet to experience a revamping like the markets of Ribeira, Campo de Ourique and Algés did, so this is the place to go if you're looking for a more traditional and neighbourhoody feel.

214 MERCADO DE ALGÉS

Rua Luís de Camões
Algés ①
www.mercado
dealges.pt

Dating from the 1950s, this is yet another of Lisbon's typical neighbourhood food markets. It was recently renovated to welcome 16 food and beverage outlets and an outdoor terrace, in addition to the traditional vendor stands. It's a lively place where you can enjoy the Lisbon way of life.

215 MERCADO 31 DE JANEIRO

Rua Engenheiro
Vieira da Silva
Saldanha ⑧
+351 21 354 0988

Located in the heart of the business district, this market offers a large variety of food vendors as well as two restaurants serving menus made with the ingredients sold in the adjoining stalls (one is vegetarian). There is also an interesting shop selling vintage furniture, an offspring of Cantinho do Vintage.

5
OLD TRADE STREETS

---

216 RUA DOS DOURADORES
Baixa ⑥

The Rua dos Douradores (Gilders' Street) used to have several shops of artisans that worked with gold, gilding frames, books or furniture. It was a craft in high demand in Old Lisbon and the Portuguese had an international reputation for doing superb gilding work.

217 RUA DOS CORREEIROS
Baixa ⑥

This is another example of a trade street that got its name after the 1755 earthquake and the following renovation of the downtown area. The *correeiros* were the city's saddlers, providing equipment for horseback riding and for the horse-drawn carriages, the main means of transport.

218 RUA DOS FANQUEIROS
Baixa ⑥

In the Rua dos Fanqueiros (Drapers' Street) not that much has changed since old times: along this Baixa street you will find dozens of shops selling fabrics for fashion and for the home. It's a very lively shopping street with shops for every budget.

219 **RUA DA PRATA**

Baixa ⑥

After the 1755 earthquake, the city's silver jewellers were concentrated along this downtown street, one of the widest in the Baixa area. These days many of those shops are still in business, some dating back to the 18th century, when silver was brought to Portugal from the mines in Brazil, a former Portuguese colony.

220 **RUA DO OURO/ RUA ÁUREA**

Baixa ⑥

Rua do Ouro (Goldsmiths' Street) was one of the trade streets that already existed before the 1755 earthquake destroyed a large part of the city. After the renovation of the city, the shops were attributed to goldsmiths and watchmakers, and later several buildings turned into bank headquarters.

The 5 best
SALONS *and*
BARBER SHOPS

---

221 PATRICK

Av. da Liberdade 245
Av. da Liberdade ④
+351 21 315 0578
*www.patrick
cabeleireiro.pt*

Brussels-born Patrick Depaus is an institution in the Lisbon hairdressing scene. When he arrived in Portugal more than 30 years ago, Patrick was among the first to establish a new generation of salons in town, bringing his artistic training into practice. The result: one of the best client lists in the city.

222 PURISTA

Rua Nova da
Trindade 16-C
Chiado ⑥
+351 91 644 2744

A groovy concept that blends a bar (specialised in craft Belgian beer) with a barbershop. The male clients can have their beard and hair trimmed day or night, while having a drink and listening to the great music selection and occasional live shows.

223 FACTO LAB

Rua do Norte 40-42
Bairro Alto ⑥
+351 21 347 8821
www.factohair.com

Facto Lab is widely regarded as one of the trendiest and most daring hairdressing salons in Lisbon, and its regular clients (many from the fashion and art world) flock to it looking for a stylish and original look. As you could expect, it's located in the heart of the avant-garde district of Bairro Alto.

224 HAIR FUSION

Travessa do Carmo 14
Chiado ⑥
+351 21 347 7302
www.hairfusion.pt

Hairstylists to the hip and famous, Joana Oliveira and Alexandre Silva are at the helm of Hair Fusion, a cool shabby-chic salon located in an old building of Chiado. They are the favourite salon of the country's top actresses and models, so you are likely to rub shoulders with a national celebrity.

225 FIGARO

Rua do Alecrim 39
Chiado ⑥
+351 21 347 0199
www.figaroslisboa.com

When this old-school barbershop opened a few years ago it created quite a stir in town because it didn't allow women inside, which led to feminist protests. Things calmed down soon after and they have been giving haircuts from the 1920s to the 1950s and razor shaves to discerning men since then.

5 neighbourhood
SHOPPING STREETS

---

226 RUA DE SÃO BENTO
Príncipe Real ⑤

This quaint shopping street is famous for its antiques dealers, with over 20 shops selling some of the best pieces in town. Must-visits are Câmara dos Pares, São Roque and Miguel Arruda. For something sweet try the ice cream at Nannarella and the chocolates at Denegro.

227 RUA DA ESCOLA POLITÉCNICA
Príncipe Real ⑤

This street in Príncipe Real is one of the hippest in town. It's always bustling with locals and visitors that browse its concept stores (Entretanto and Embaixada), antiques dealers, restaurants (Zero Zero, Prego da Peixaria). Also the Botanical Garden and the Natural History Museum are here.

228 RUA GARRETT
Chiado ⑥

The back bone of Chiado, Rua Garrett is home to some of the city's best cafes, boutiques, bookshops (Bertrand, Sá da Costa), traditional shops (Casa Pereira, Paris em Lisboa), a small shopping mall and also flagship outlets of global brands like Nespresso, Boss, Swarovski or Tous.

229 **AVENIDA DE ROMA**

Avenidas Novas ⑧

Avenida de Roma in the Alvalade district is one of the main thoroughfares that were built in the early 20th century as part of the city's expansion. It is the epicentre of northern Lisbon and a great place to visit if you want to experience authentic local life without tourists around.

230 **RUA FERREIRA BORGES**

Campo de Ourique ③

This tree-lined street is famous for its shops and cafes. People from all over the city come here to unwind and feel the warmness of Campo de Ourique, Lisbon's locals' favourite neighbourhood. Have a coffee on the outdoor terrace of Tentadora before visiting the many interesting shops around.

228 **RUA GARRETT**

The 5 best shops for
ANTIQUES

---

231 LIVRARIA CAMPOS TRINDADE

Rua do Alecrim 44
Chiado ⑥
+351 21 347 1857
www.livraria
campostrindade.com

This treasure chest of old books is a second-generation family business, opened in the 70s by current owner Bernardo Trindade's father. It is probably the best place in town to discover literary rarities and Bernardo is always there to guide the eye. Even if you don't buy anything, the shop is pure bliss to visit.

232 D'OREY TILES

Rua do Alecrim 68
Chiado ⑥
+351 21 343 0232
www.doreytiles.pt

Glazed tiles (*azulejos*) have been a prized tradition in Portugal since the long Moorish occupation, which lasted seven centuries and ended in 1250. This shop is the best in town for *azulejos* and their selection encompasses many centuries, from Moorish inspired designs, to baroque and even more contemporary ones.

233 JORGE WELSH

Rua da
Misericórdia 43
Chiado ⑥
+351 21 395 3375
www.jorgewelsh.com

Jorge Welsh is one of the world's leading experts in Chinese porcelain and his sleek and sophisticated shop in Chiado (he owns another one in London) holds a more valuable collection than many museums. If you are passionate about porcelain from the Far East this extraordinary shop is your dream come true.

234 SÃO ROQUE

R. de São Bento 269
Príncipe Real ⑤
+351 21 397 0197
www.antiguida
dessaoroque.com

Lisbon's best antiques dealer has two exquisite shops in Rua de São Bento: São Roque and São Roque Too. Both of them display pieces collected by the owner, Mário Roque. It is by far the best selection of antiques and modern art available in the city.

235 MIGUEL ARRUDA

R. de São Bento 356
Príncipe Real ⑤
+351 21 396 1165
www.arruda.pt

Miguel Arruda also owns an auction house giving him the opportunity to buy world-class pieces for his antiques shop located in an 18th-century building in São Bento. There he showcases ancient furniture, religious art, old masters' paintings, porcelain and silverware.

The 5 best
CONCEPT STORES

---

236 SKINLIFE

Rua Paiva de
Andrade 4-4A
Chiado ⑥
+351 21 193 0236
www.skinlife.pt

Dutch couple Dennis and Patrick own this unique perfume and cosmetics concept store in Chiado. The beautifully designed shop sells their exquisite selection of exclusive labels and signature lines of skincare, hair and make-up products.

237 EMBAIXADA

Praça do Príncipe
Real 26
Príncipe Real ⑤
+351 96 530 9154
www.embaixadalx.pt

Occupying a picturesque neo-Moorish palace from the 1800s, this shopping gallery is in fact a large concept store with about a dozen different shops that are spread over the two floors of the building. There are also some restaurants and an outdoor terrace.

238 CASA PAU-BRASIL

Rua da Escola
Politécnica 42
Príncipe Real ⑤
+351 21 342 0954

This concept store, housed in the Castilho Palace, is truly unique. It holds several small shops, each of them in a different room of the palace. Every little shop represents a brand from Brasil, in diverse areas: there's Brazilian fashion (Lenny, Juliana Herc), beauty (Granado), furniture (Campana Brothers) and food (Chocolates Q).

239 LOJA REAL

Praça do Príncipe
Real 20
Príncipe Real ⑤
+351 21 346 1147
www.loja-real.com

Loja Real started out as a shop selling upscale children's clothes and then gradually added clothing and shoes for women and men to the selection, as well as gadgets, books, toys and home décor pieces.

240 21PR CONCEPT STORE

Praça do Príncipe
Real 21
Príncipe Real ⑤
+351 21 346 9421

This concept store, that was set up by local fashion designer Ricardo Preto, is a showroom of design brands, some Portuguese, some international. Now you will find five shops-in-a-shop here, selling homemade chocolates, women's fashion, jewellery, home décor and gourmet goods.

FUNDAÇÃO CHAMPALIMAUD

25 BUILDINGS
TO ADMIRE

———

The 5 most striking
HISTORIC BUILDINGS

---

241 MOSTEIRO DOS JERÓNIMOS

Praça do Império
Belém ②
+351 21 362 0034
*www.mosteiro
jeronimos.pt*

This UNESCO World Heritage Site was built in the 16th century, in the rich and ornate Manueline style. It's the finest illustration of the power and wealth of the Portuguese nation during the Age of Discovery. Don't miss the tombs of Vasco da Gama and Luís de Camões.

242 TORRE DE BELÉM

Avenida Brasília
Belém ②
+351 21 362 0034
www.torrebelem.pt

Torre de Belém (a World Heritage Site) is unarguably the most beautiful historical prison facility in the world, even if it was originally built (in 1515) for the military defence of the city. It's Lisbon's most significant landmark, an icon of the city and of Portugal as well.

243 ESTAÇÃO DO ROSSIO

Rua 1º de Dezembro
Baixa ⑥

Lisbon's historical central station, built in the palatial Neo-Manueline style, is probably one of the most beautiful railway stations in the world. Recent renovations have given it back all its grandeur while creating spaces for offices, restaurants and a hostel.

244 **CONVENTO DO CARMO**

Largo do Carmo
Chiado ⑥
+351 21 347 8629

The dramatic ruins of the Gothic Carmo Convent are one the few visible reminders of the daunting 1st November 1755, when a gigantic earthquake and tsunami virtually destroyed the city. The convent church stood ground but lost its roof, which was never replaced.

245 **SÉ DE LISBOA**

Largo da Sé
Sé ⑦
+351 21 886 6752
www.patriarcado-lisboa.pt

Lisbon's Sé cathedral, built in the 1100s, is the city's finest remaining example of the Romanesque architectural style. With defensive towers and battlements it looks more like a castle than a church. It holds a myriad of treasures, including royal tombs, a famous nativity scene and a Gothic period cloister.

242 **TORRE DE BELÉM**

The 5 most
UNIQUE MONUMENTS

---

246 PANTEÃO NACIONAL

Campo de
Santa Clara
Graça ⑦
+351 21 885 4820

Portugal's National Pantheon is the final destination of the most important political and artistic personalities in the country. Its 'residents' include several former presidents, poets and writers, fado legend Amália Rodrigues and, more recently, football player Eusébio. (Yes, the Portuguese really do love football…)

247 CRISTO REI

Alto do Pragal,
Avenida Cristo Rei
Almada ①
+351 21 275 1000
www.cristorei.pt

This monument was inaugurated in 1959 as a symbol of the Portuguese Catholic Church's appreciation and gratitude to God for sparing Lisbon of the drama of the Second World War. It stands 75 metres tall to offer the most phenomenal view of the city and the Tagus. The panorama is well worth the trip across the river.

248 AQUEDUTO DAS ÁGUAS LIVRES

Calçada da
Quintinha 6
Campolide ④
+351 21 810 0215

Lisbon's remarkable aqueduct was built in the 1700s as a means of bringing fresh water into the city. The modern development of the city has demolished most of its structures but some can still be seen in various places around the city and particularly in the valley of Campolide, where the tallest section still stands tall and awes passers-by.

249 PRAÇA DE TOUROS DO CAMPO PEQUENO

Avenidas Novas ⑧
+351 21 799 8450
*www.campo
pequeno.com*

Lisbon has one of the most stunning and original bullfighting rings in the world, rivaling with those of Sevilla and Ronda. Built in the 19th century with a Neo-Moorish inspiration, it is still the stage for bullfights, a strong yet controversial Portuguese cultural tradition. A few years ago a shopping arcade was built on the lower floors.

250 PADRÃO DOS DESCOBRIMENTOS

Avenida Brasília
Belém ②
+351 21 303 1950
*www.padraodos
descobrimentos.pt*

This bold landmark that stands proudly on the riverside, is a symbol of the Age of the Discovery. It pays tribute to Prince Henry the Navigator and the sailors and explorers that sailed the world under his patronage, bringing unseen prosperity to Portugal. An elevator takes visitors to the top, where a viewpoint offers stunning views.

5 stunning
MODERN BUILDINGS

---

251 PAVILHÃO DE PORTUGAL
Parque das Nações,
Alameda dos Oceanos
Parque das Nações ⑩

Pritzker Prize winner Siza Vieira designed this iconic pavilion for the 1998 World Fair – for this occasion a new city was created in the shabby-industrial eastern part of Lisbon. The most impressive feature of the pavilion is the immense concrete roof, which seems as light as a feather, challenging gravity in the eye of the beholder.

252 TORRE DE CONTROLO DO PORTO DE LISBOA
Belém ②

When you enter Lisbon coming from the sea, the first thing to catch your eye is the leaning port control tower, designed by local architect Gonçalo Byrne. The audacious building, that far exceeds its functional purpose thanks to its beauty, has won several architectural awards, and is the perfect contemporary companion for the other riverside monuments.

255 **FUNDAÇÃO CHAMPALIMAUD**

252 **TORRE DE CONTROLO DO PORTO DE LISBOA**

253 EDP HEADQUARTERS

Avenida 24 de Julho
Cais do Sodré ⑥

This light and airy building was designed by award-winning architecture firm Aires Mateus as the headquarters of the former state-owned energy company EDP. Located next door to the Mercado da Ribeira it blends perfectly with the contrasting surroundings, despite its size and style. It has in fact set a new standard for contemporary architecture in the city.

254 MUSEU DOS COCHES

Praça Afonso de
Albuquerque
Belém ②
+351 21 361 0850
*www.museu
doscoches.pt*

The new Museu dos Coches was designed by Brazilian Pritzker Prize winner Paulo Mendes da Rocha on a plot adjacent to the old museum, that used to be occupied by the former royal riding school. The museum offers an interesting contemporary backdrop to the richly decorated carriages, some of which date as far back as the 15th century.

255 FUNDAÇÃO CHAMPALIMAUD

Centro
Champalimaud,
Avenida de Brasília
Belém ②
+351 21 048 0200
*www.fchampali
maud.org*

The Champalimaud Centre for the Unknown is housed in a state-of-the-art building designed by Indian architect Charles Correa. Located on the riverbank, near the mouth of the Tagus, the building finds the perfect balance between form and function. It truly expresses the essence of the magnificent location it was built on.

5

REMARKABLE PALACES

256 CASA DO ALENTEJO

Rua das Portas de
Santo Antão 58
Av. da Liberdade ④
+351 21 340 5140
*www.casado
alentejo.com.pt*

It's hard to imagine the wonders that are kept inside of the Casa do Alentejo. The interiors are of Neo-Moorish inspiration, with richly decorated palatial rooms, a restaurant and a grand hall that is the perfect décor for the social functions and cultural events that take place regularly.

257 PALÁCIO FOZ

Praça dos
Restauradores
Av. da Liberdade ④
+351 21 322 1200
*www.gmcs.pt/
palaciofoz*

This palace (which can only be visited by groups with a reservation) was built in the late 1700s and shows a blend of several architectural styles, from baroque to Neo-Manueline. Its rooms rival in grandeur with those of the royal palace.

258 PALÁCIO DA AJUDA

Largo da Ajuda
Ajuda ①
+351 21 363 7095
www.palacioajuda.pt

After the big 1755 earthquake and tsunami that destroyed the royal palace located on the riverfront, the royal family decided to build a new palace on a hopefully safer, higher ground above Belém. The palace was never fully completed but the existing part is worth a visit because of the richness of the décor and the grandeur of the rooms.

259 CASTELO DE SÃO JORGE

Rua de Santa
Cruz do Castelo
Castelo ⑦
+351 21 880 0620
*www.castelode
saojorge.pt*

The history of Lisbon is that of its castle, which stands on a vantage point, high above all the other hills of the city. The oldest archaeological findings date from the 6th century, thus the castle is about 1500 years old. It was a royal residence until the royal family moved to the palace of Ribeira in the 16th century.

260 ASSEMBLEIA DA REPÚBLICA

Palácio de São Bento
Lapa ③
+351 21 391 9000
www.parlamento.pt

The Portuguese National Assembly (Palace of São Bento) occupies a former 16th-century monastery that was desecrated and transformed into a neoclassical palace. It is open for visits and you can even attend the parliamentary sessions if you are at all curious about how politics are conducted in Portugal.

259 CASTELO DE SÃO JORGE

5 special
LIFTS *and* ELEVATORS

261 ASCENSOR DA GLÓRIA
Calçada da Glória
Chiado ⑥

The electrical Ascensor da Glória (Glória funicular) dates from 1885 and offers a 275-metre ride between the garden of São Pedro de Alcântara and the square of Restauradores, helping pedestrians go up the strenuous 18-degree slope. The slope, and the funicular itself, serve as an urban canvas for the city's graffiti artists.

262 ASCENSOR DA BICA
Rua da Bica de
Duarte Belo
Cais do Sodré ⑥

The Bica funicular is the most picturesque in Lisbon. The ride takes people up and down the much-photographed Rua da Bica de Duarte Belo, from São Paulo street to Calçada do Combro and Chiado. A hotel opened in the building where the funicular departs from. At night the funicular doesn't run; that's when the street's bars open their doors and the atmosphere becomes truly magical.

262 ASCENSOR DA BICA

263 ELEVADOR DE SANTA JUSTA

Rua Áurea
Chiado ⑥
+351 21 413 8679

This stunning 45-metre long neo-Gothic vertical lift was built to bring people back and forth between downtown and Chiado. Many attribute it to Gustave Eiffel, but in fact the father of the Eiffel Tower didn't design it. At the very top there is a terrace with a mind-blowing 360-degree view of the old city. Beware of pickpockets when going up the spiral staircase.

264 CHÃO DO LOUREIRO AND CASTELO

Mercado do
Chão do Loureiro
Baixa ⑥

These two vertical lifts make the walk from the downtown area to the Castle a little less tiring. The first lift departs from a building in Rua dos Fanqueiros (170/178) and drops people off in Rua da Madalena. A mere 100 metres further there is another lift, that transports passengers to the level of Costa do Castelo street.

265 ASCENSOR DO LAVRA

Calçada do Lavra
Av. da Liberdade ④
+351 21 413 8681

This was the city's first funicular. It started taking passengers from Av. da Liberdade up Calçada do Lavra in 1884, a year before the Glória funicular came into operation. Like the other traditional funiculars and lifts in Lisbon, it is classified as a National Monument.

JARDIM BOTÂNICO

50 PLACES
TO DISCOVER
LISBON

The 5 best
VIEWS IN LISBON

---

266 JARDIM AMÁLIA RODRIGUES
Alameda Cardeal Cerejeira
Parque Eduardo VII ④

Jardim Amália Rodrigues might very well be the highest natural viewpoint in Lisbon. The garden overlooks the entire city and offers an unobstructed view of the Eduardo VII Park, Marquês de Pombal square and Av. da Liberdade. On a clear day you can see as far as the Arrábida mountains and Palmela.

267 MIRADOURO DE SÃO PEDRO DE ALCÂNTARA
Rua São Pedro de Alcântara
Chiado ⑥

De São Pedro Alcântara garden has the best location in town, on the confluence of Chiado, Príncipe Real and Bairro Alto. It offers a 180-degree panorama of the downtown area, the Castle, Graça hill, and the river. There are two levels, the top one with trees and a kiosk and the lower one with beautiful French-style gardens.

268 ARCO DA RUA AUGUSTA

267 MIRADOURO DE SÃO PEDRO DE ALCÂNTARA

268 ARCO DA RUA AUGUSTA

Rua Augusta 2
Baixa ⑥

The triumphal arch at the start of Rua Augusta was built in 1875 to serve as the gateway to the city as you approach it from the river. The arch has a terrace up top that can be reached by elevator and from where you can experience one of the most unique 360-degree views of Lisbon.

269 SANTA CATARINA

Largo de Santa Catarina
Santa Catarina ⑤

The Santa Catarina viewpoint is located in the charming quarter with the same name, surrounded by palaces and luxury apartments. It's a very relaxed place, where you will always find street musicians and artists, youngsters drinking in groups and people enjoying the wide river views. There are a couple of cool kiosks and bars around.

270 PORTAS DO SOL

Largo Portas do Sol
Alfama ⑦

This mirador's name translates to 'Sun Doors' and it makes perfect sense: this is the best place in town to watch the sunrise. The superb panoramic views grasp all of the Alfama quarter with its traditional brick-coloured rooftops, the monastery of Saint Vincent, and the river. Grab a seat at the kiosk or the terrace cafe and enjoy the scenery.

5 places to
UNDERSTAND THE
HISTORY OF LISBON

---

271 BAIXA POMBALINA
Baixa ⑥

Downtown Lisbon (Baixa) was completely rebuilt after the 1755 earthquake. The then prime minister, the Marquis of Pombal, redesigned the city to prepare it for the future, with wider avenues, some of which were consigned to pedestrian traffic only.

272 LISBON STORY CENTER
Terreiro do Paço 78 81
Baixa ⑥
+351 21 194 1099
*www.lisboastory
centre.pt*

This themed museum opened a few years ago in the east wing of Terreiro do Paço. The multimedia and multisensory experience tells the story of the city and of its most significant events and personalities. There is a gift shop selling Lisbon merchandising.

273 LARGO DO CARMO
Largo do Carmo
Chiado ⑥

This is where you'll find the ruins of the Carmo Convent and it was also here that the 1974 peaceful Revolution of the Carnations started, when the military surrounded the police headquarters where the prime minister had taken refuge, before he was forced to resign.

274 MUSEU DA CIDADE

Campo Grande 245
Avenidas Novas ⑧
+351 21 751 3200
www.museudelisboa.pt

The Lisbon Museum takes an original approach to museology by being a multi-branched museum with five venues: Palácio Pimenta, Teatro Romano, Santo António, Torreão Poente and Casa dos Bicos. All of these branches together tell the story of this surprising city's past.

275 PALÁCIO DE BELÉM

Palácio de Belém
Calçada da Ajuda
Belém ②
+351 21 361 4600
www.presidencia.pt

The Belém Palace, the official residence of the Portuguese president, ironically served as a royal residence at a certain point in time. The points of interest include the beautifully landscaped gardens and the Museum of the Presidency, that tells the story of the Portuguese republic through its presidents.

271 BAIXA POMBALINA

5 of the best places to
ENJOY THE RIVER

---

276 **CAIS DO GINJAL**
Rua do Ginjal
Cacilhas
Almada ⓘ

The Cais do Ginjal is located on the other side of the river and it's accessible by taking the ferry that departs from Cais do Sodré to Cacilhas. The trip across the river is a great experience in itself but the cherry on the cake is walking along the river with Lisbon as scenery. There are a few restaurants on the boardwalk with stunning views.

277 **PASSEIO DAS DOCAS**
Doca de
Santo Amaro
Alcântara ⓘ
+351 21 392 2011

The lively Lisbon docks, located right under the bridge, are basically a series of reconverted warehouses that now house a multitude of restaurants, cafes and nightclubs. There is something happening here every hour of the day. The marina in front is a pleasant place and there are also several paddle tennis courts.

278 PARQUE DO TEJO

Parque das Nações
Parque das Nações ⑩
*www.portaldas
nacoes.pt*

This waterfront park is popular with residents of eastern Lisbon who go there on weekends to walk, run or cycle, while enjoying the views of the Vasco da Gama bridge and the tower. If you bring a pair of binoculars you might spot aquatic birds and even flamingos that reside in the Tagus estuary during certain months of the year.

279 BELÉM

Belém ②

The promenade between the 25th of April bridge and Belém is a favourite with locals, who are to be found there every day of the week jogging, cycling, fishing, walking their dogs or simply enjoying the river views with their loved ones. Along the promenade there are several lawns and terraces where you can relax while gazing at the scenery.

280 RIBEIRA DAS NAUS

Ribeira das Naus
Baixa ⑥

This boardwalk links the Terreiro do Paço square to Cais do Sodré. It was opened in 2013, and it's the nicest place to enjoy the river in old Lisbon. The area was a naval shipyard during the Age of Discovery and it was here that the ships sailed off to the Portuguese lands overseas. On warmer days hundreds of people lie on the grass enjoying the sun.

5
HIDDEN CHURCHES

---

281 ERMIDA DE BELÉM
Travessa do
Marta Pinto 21
Belém ②
+351 21 363 7700
*www.travessa
daermida.com*

This tiny 18th-century former chapel
is truly a hidden secret. It houses an
innovative cultural initiative, including
a contemporary art and design exhibition
space, a wine bar, and a jewellery
workshop. The narrow street where it's
located is part of the project.

282 CAPELA DE SANTO AMARO
Calçada de Santo
Amaro
Alcântara ①

This very discreet and unimposing chapel
located at the very top of the Santo Amaro
hill is a national monument, so it is by
definition worth a visit. It dates from
1549, and it's shaped in a very original
circular form. The *azulejos* (glazed tiles)
are outstanding and so is the view.

283 CAPELA DA ORDEM TERCEIRA DO CARMO
Largo do Carmo
Rua Oliveira do
Carmo 4
Chiado ⑥
+351 21 342 1790
*www.ordem-do-
carmo.pt*

You can pass by the square of Carmo
every day of your life and never notice
this stunning intimate chapel, located
on the first floor of the building that
houses the religious Order of Carmo.
To visit it, just walk through the doors,
climb the stone staircase and be dazzled
by the ornate gilded altar piece that's
hidden inside.

284 IGREJA DA CONCEIÇÃO VELHA

Rua da
Alfândega 108
Baixa ⑥
+351 21 887 0202

The church of Conceição Velha (also a national monument) was built in 1496 on the ruins of the Jewish synagogue that once stood there. The church was destroyed during the 1755 earthquake, but it was rebuilt with parts of other churches, which explains its anachronistic Manueline-style façade. Inside is a valuable collection of religious paintings.

285 ERMIDA DO RESTELO

Jardim Ducla Soares
Belém ②

The Ermida do Restelo (a national monument) stands high above the Belém quarter overlooking the avenue that leads to the Tower of Belém. It dates from the 15th century and is said to have welcomed Vasco da Gama and his men for a night of prayers before they departed on their expedition to the Orient in 1497.

The 5 best
TRAM, BUS *and* BOAT
rides

---

286 **TRAFARIA PRAIA**

Joana Vasconcelos, Portugal's leading contemporary artist, created Trafaria Praia for the Venice Biennale as an allegorical blend of the iconic Lisbon ferryboat, the *cacilheiro*, and the Venetian vaporetto. Vasconcelos' floating artwork is now docked in Lisbon and is open for visits and river cruises.

287 **CACILHEIRO**

Cacilheiros are the boats that connect the two banks of the Tagus. As the name hints, they originally linked Lisbon to Cacilhas, but now there are more routes. The trip is phenomenal and lets visitors experience Lisbon in a different way.

288 **NUMBER 28 TRAM**

A ride with the number 28 tram (7 kilometres in total) is probably Lisbon's most popular tourist activity. The tram takes passengers from Campo de Ourique to Martim Moniz, going up and down the hills and passing by the city's major points of interest. Beware of pickpockets on the tram.

289 CORK TRAM

Enjoy a ride on any of the two trams that have been completely recovered and lined in cork, a very important product for the Portuguese economy (Portugal is the biggest producer of cork in the world). The 'Eletri'Cork' trams rides in the historic centre, from Figueira Square to the Castle of São Jorge.

290 HIPPOTRIP
www.hippotrip.com

The HIPPOtrip bus/boat offers a funky and adventurous Lisbon sightseeing experience aboard amphibious vehicles that take passengers on a 90-minute trip around the city by land and… river. During the tour the lively animators will entertain passengers while sharing historical facts and stories about the places they pass by.

288 NUMBER 28 TRAM

5 great
NEIGHBOURHOODS

291 **CAMPO DE OURIQUE**
Campo de Ourique ③

This residential and commercial neighbourhood is a locals' favourite. They go there to shop for food or children's clothing, and to enjoy its many restaurants. It lies somewhat away from the main tourist attractions in the city (but it is the last/first stop of the 28 tram), which is one more reason to go there and experience the real Lisbon.

292 **PRÍNCIPE REAL**
Príncipe Real ⑤

This enchanting neighbourhood lines the north part of Bairro Alto and over the course of the last ten years it has become the city's top destination for contemporary shopping and cool restaurants. It has a perfect mixture of public and residential buildings and some offices, pleasant gardens and an upscale atmosphere.

293 CHIADO

Chiado ⑥

This has been Lisbon's most sophisticated district for over 150 years, where local trendsetters go for shopping, culture, entertainment and food. Many buildings in Chiado were severely damaged in a major fire in the 1990s and underwent a substantial restoration under the supervision of award-winning architect Álvaro Siza Vieira.

294 ALFAMA

Alfama ⑦

Alfama is perhaps Lisbon's oldest quarter (the second oldest neighbourhood in Europe), dating from the earliest settlements of the city. It has the atmosphere of a rural village inside the city; quaint, traditional, shabby and with a certain medieval feel. It's a place to discover on foot, letting yourself get lost in the labyrinth of streets, squares and alleys.

295 BAIRRO ALTO

Bairro Alto ⑥

Bairro Alto ('High Quarter') is a groovy neighbourhood that has always been Lisbon's nightlife district, filled with all kinds of restaurants and bars. During the day life passes by at a slower pace; there are many small hipster boutiques and shops here, and art galleries and cafes, attracting both the older residents and the younger bohemian ones.

296 JARDIM BOTÂNICO TROPICAL

Largo dos Jerónimos
Belém ②

This gem of a garden in Belém was created in the early 1900s as a botanical showcase of the wonders existing in the former Portuguese colonies in Africa and Asia (over 4000 species were planted here), with a special emphasis on plants from Macau. It's a delightful retreat in the city, ideal for a leisurely walk in nature.

297 JARDIM BOTÂNICO DE LISBOA

Rua da Escola
Politécnica 54
Príncipe Real ⑤
+351 21 392 1800
www.museus.ulisboa.pt/ jardim-botanico

Tucked away behind the Museum of Natural History, this stunning four-hectare garden is easily overlooked by people walking around Príncipe Real. Its heyday, when it was considered one of the best in Europe, has long gone and now the garden is a bit run-down but it does have a nice, sort of mystical feel.

298 JARDIM BOTÂNICO DA AJUDA

Calçada da Ajuda
Ajuda ①
+351 21 362 2503
*www.jardimbotanico
dajuda.com*

Built in 1768 as part of the adjoining royal palace of Ajuda, this beautifully manicured garden was the city's first botanical garden. The most noteworthy parts are the French-style box gardens, the exotic tree species (most of them originating from Portugal's former colonies) and a delicate Rococo fountain.

299 JARDIM GULBENKIAN

Av. de Berna 45-A
Avenidas Novas ⑧
+351 217 82 3000
*www.gulbenkian.pt/
Jardins*

This is the best example of modernistic landscaping in Lisbon. Designed in the 60s by the 20th century's leading Portuguese landscape architect Gonçalo Ribeiro Telles, the garden covers an entire city block and is full of hidden corners and micro-landscapes where visitors can get away from the city noise.

300 JARDIM DA ESTRELA

Praça da Estrela
Estrela ③
+351 21 397 4818
*jardimdaestrela.
no.sapo.pt*

Across the street from the Basílica da Estrela, this garden offers a lovely and quiet atmosphere, perfect for relaxing, jogging or having a picnic. There's a large children's playground, a couple of kiosks, a pond and a stunning 19th-century bandstand.

5
SMALL SQUARES

---

301 PRAÇA DAS AMOREIRAS
Praça das Amoreiras
Amoreiras ④

The intimately small square is right in the centre of the city but the feel is almost rural, as if you were transported to a village in the countryside, far away from the traffic and noise of the city. The garden that occupies the square is lined with trees and has a lively kiosk and an art museum.

302 LARGO DO CARMO
Chiado ⑥

The Carmo square is the calmest spot in Chiado, far from the busy streets of this elegant district. It has restaurants with outdoor terraces, a kiosk, a museum and a church. It is also the entry point to the lift of Santa Justa and to the viewpoint of the Carmo terraces.

303 LARGO DE SÃO PAULO
Largo de São Paulo
Cais do Sodré ⑥

This Parisian-style square located in the lower part of the city, at the river level, was for many decades a shabby area where you really wouldn't feel comfortable at night, given the many illegal activities that went on there. Now all that has changed and the square and the adjoining streets are the heart of Lisbon's nightlife.

304 LARGO DE SÃO MIGUEL

Largo de São Miguel
Alfama ⑦

This closed square is where you'll find the imposing church of São Miguel, with its steps where people sit on warm nights drinking and enjoying the scenery. You'll also find many fado restaurants here that provide a lively soundtrack to the daily life of the square's residents and visitors.

305 LARGO DA PARADA

Rua 4 de Infantaria
Campo de Ourique ③

Largo da Parada lies in an easy-going part of town, in a quarter that's appreciated by locals for its shopping opportunities and family feel. It's a nice place to observe the local residents living their daily lives.

303 LARGO DE SÃO PAULO

The 5 most
PEACEFUL SPOTS

---

306 TAPADA DAS NECESSIDADES
Largo Necessidades 58
Lapa ③

The garden of the Ministry of Foreign Affairs really is a hidden secret. It's open to visitors but often completely deserted, even during weekends. It's an enchanting park to get away from it all and enjoy nature, lying down on the wide lawn or resting under the shade of exotic trees.

307 TAPADA DA AJUDA
Tapada da Ajuda
Ajuda ①
+351 21 365 3100

This large state-owned estate is part of the Agricultural School and its grounds are used by students to plant crops as part of their training. There are surprising viewpoints where you can enjoy the river without any tourists around.

308 PARQUE FLORESTAL DE MONSANTO
Monsanto

This enormous urban forest serves as the city's lungs. It is a place where locals go to enjoy the outdoors, walking or jogging on the pine-tree-lined paths. There are plenty of leisure and sports areas, which include a tennis club, rugby and football fields, children's playgrounds, and many picnic areas.

309 **JARDIM DO TOREL**

Rua Julio de
Andrade
Av. da Liberdade ④

Nestled high above Av. da Liberdade (you can get here by the Lavra funicular) and overlooking the west side of town, the Torel garden remains a hidden treasure even for locals. The garden has an intimate terrace cafe, and in August the municipality installs a large pool here called Torel's beach.

310 **MUSEU DO TEATRO E TRAJE**

Largo Júlio Castilho
Lumiar ⑧
+351 21 756 7620
www.museudotraje.pt

This unexpected museum duo shares a small secluded botanical garden from the 1800s. Visitors love its peaceful atmosphere and its many interesting botanical species. It's a bit far from the centre but well worth the detour: who wouldn't enjoy the privilege of having a garden almost all to oneself?

306 TAPADA DAS NECESSIDADES

5
INTERESTING CEMETERIES

---

311 **PET CEMETERY**
Lisbon Zoo
Sete Rios

This pet cemetery is located on a terraced hillside in the Lisbon Zoo, and dates back to the 1940s. There aren't any new burials here these days but it's interesting to see the tombs that owners made for their loved (four-legged) ones, some in marble, others covered with traditional Portuguese tiles.

312 **CEMITÉRIO DOS PRAZERES**
Praça São João Bosco
Campo de Ourique ③

Located in Campo de Ourique in front of the last/first stop of tram 28, the cemetery of Prazeres was installed in the early 1800s to bury the many victims of a cholera epidemic. Later it became the preferred burial ground of Lisbon's wealthiest families, who built very ornate and rich tombs and mausoleums.

313 CEMITÉRIO DO ALTO DE SÃO JOÃO

Parada Alto de São João
Alto de São João ⑨

Built in the beginning of the 9th century, this cemetery occupies a large area overlooking the Madredeus district and was created for the deceased residents of eastern Lisbon. It has many paths filled with rich mausoleums that show the wealth of it residents. Portuguese Nobel Prize winner José Saramago was buried here.

314 ENGLISH CEMETERY

Avenida de Álvares Cabral
Estrela ③

A treaty between Lord Cromwell and King João the Fourth, signed in 1654, determines that English men and women living in Portugal should have a plot 'fit for the burial of their dead'. The anti-Anglican Inquisition opposed; that's why the St. George's cemetery was only built in 1717.

315 GERMAN CEMETERY

Rua do Patrocínio 59
Campo de Ourique ③

The first reports of Germans being buried in Lisbon date from 1147, when during the Second Crusade German knights fought in Lisbon's siege and perished here. In 1821 a wealthy German businessman donated a plot of land to the local German community in the quarter of Campo de Ourique. It is open for visits by appointment.

MUSEU DO AZULEJO

75 PLACES TO ENJOY CULTURE

The 5 best
SMALL MUSEUMS

———————

316 MUSEU GEOLÓGICO
Rua da Academia das Ciências 19 – 2°
Príncipe Real ⑤
+351 21 346 3915
www.lneg.pt/
museugeologico

This hidden museum in a quiet street of Príncipe Real holds an outstanding collection of fossils and stratified rocks, with a notable display of minerals from Portugal and abroad. Its use of historical exhibition furniture also makes it a 'museum of museums', where you will be swept away by much more than just its collection.

317 MUSEU BORDALO PINHEIRO
Campo Grande 382
Avenidas Novas ⑧
+351 21 817 0667
www.museubordalo
pinheiro.cm-lisboa.pt

Bordallo Pinheiro was one of the most remarkable personalities of the Portuguese cultural scene of the 1900s. He worked in different artistic fields, from plastic arts to graphic arts, from decorative arts to ceramics – the latter being the area in which he gained the most accolades. The museum displays a wide selection of his works.

318 MUSEU FUNDAÇÃO MEDEIROS E ALMEIDA

Rua Rosa Araújo 41
Av. da Liberdade ④
+351 21 354 7892
www.casa-museu
medeirosealmeida.pt

The former palatial residence of António de Medeiros e Almeida (a wealthy businessman) now houses its founder's prized collection of paintings, Chinese porcelain, ancient clocks and French furniture. Among the many valuable pieces are paintings by Rembrandt, Rubens and Tiepolo.

319 MUSEU DE ETNOLOGIA

Avenida Ilha da Madeira
Belém ②
+351 21 304 1160
www.mnetnologia.
wordpress.com

The National Museum of Ethnology is the repository of the country's national collections of African, Asian and South American tribal art, formed during the centuries that the Portuguese had colonies on those continents. The museum also showcases artifacts that shed light on the culture and lifestyle of Portugal's rural areas.

320 MUSEU DE HISTÓRIA NATURAL

Rua da Escola Politécnica 56-58
Príncipe Real ⑤
+351 21 392 1800
www.museus.
ulisboa.pt

The National Museum of Natural History and Science is the country's most pre-eminent cultural institution dedicated to the study of Nature. Its rich collections, built up over 300 years, encompass the fields of geology, anthropology and botany. The museum complex also includes the city's Botanical Garden.

The 5 best MODERN and CONTEMPORARY ART MUSEUMS

---

321 MUSEU NATIONAL DE ARTE CONTEMPORÂNEO DO CHIADO

Rua Serpa Pinto 4
Chiado ⑥
+351 21 343 2148
www.museu
artecontemporanea.pt

This secluded museum in Chiado has a very representative collection of modern and contemporary Portuguese art on display, from the late 1800s to today, with significant artworks by artists like Amadeo de Souza-Cardoso, Columbano Bordalo Pinheiro, Almada Negreiros, Silva Porto, Mario Cesariny and Paula Rego.

322 CENTRO DE ARTE MODERNA

Rua Dr. Nicolau de Bettencourt
Avenidas Novas ⑧
+351 21 782 3474
www.cam.
gulbenkian.pt

Part of the marvelous Calouste Gulbenkian Foundation, this Centre for Modern Art exhibits a permanent collection of Portuguese and International art, including works by Lourdes Castro, Amadeo de Souza-Cardoso, Paula Rego and David Hockney. The gardens around the museum are an oasis of peace in the city.

323 MUSEU COLEÇÃO BERARDO

323 MUSEU COLEÇÃO BERARDO

**Praça do Império
Belém ②
+351 21 361 2878
*www.museuberardo.pt***

Throughout the years, controversial businessman Joe Berardo built up an impressive collection of modern and contemporary art and stored it at the Centro Cultural de Belém. The Museu Berardo is part of the CCB, it is housed there, inside the CCB. The Berardo Museum displays works by Joana Vasconcelos, Miró, Warhol, Picasso, Schnabel and Basquiat, and has regular and noteworthy temporary exhibits.

324 MUSEU VIEIRA DA SILVA-ARPAD SZENES

**Praça das
Amoreiras 56
Amoreiras ④
+351 21 388 0044
*www.fasvs.pt***

A former royal silk factory in the charming garden of Amoreiras now houses an intimate museum dedicated to Portugal's greatest 20th-century artist, Vieira da Silva, and to her husband Arpad Szenes. The museum hosts interesting temporary exhibitions and cultural initiatives.

325 ATELIER MUSEU JÚLIO POMAR

**Rua do Vale 7
Príncipe Real ⑤
+351 21 588 0793
*www.ateliermuseu
juliopomar.pt***

This small and very unknown museum is solely dedicated to the preservation and promotion of the work of Júlio Pomar, one of the most important Portuguese artists of the 20th century. It is housed in a former warehouse redesigned by architect Siza Vieira and holds an impressive number of Pomar's works.

The 5 most inspiring
CULTURAL VENUES

---

326 **CCB**
Praça do Império
Belém ②
+351 21 361 2400
www.ccb.pt

This large multi-purpose centre is home to a number of cultural venues including Lisbon's biggest concert hall, a contemporary art museum, a conference centre, a cafe and a restaurant, and a series of art galleries and shops. It hosts regular world-class theatre and ballet performances and a lot of concerts.

327 **TEATRO NACIONAL D. MARIA II**
Praça Dom Pedro IV
Baixa ⑥
+351 21 325 0800
www.teatro-dmaria.pt

The imposing façade of the neoclassical Dona Maria II National Theatre stands on Rossio square, in the very heart of the city. Inside the sumptuous building there are two theatre rooms from where the National Theatre Company operates and where mostly classical plays are staged, both by Portuguese and international playwrights.

328 TEATRO NACIONAL DE SÃO CARLOS

Rua Serpa Pinto 9
Chiado ⑥
+351 21 325 3000
www.tnsc.pt

The São Carlos National Theatre was built after the earthquake of 1755, which destroyed the previous opera house, Europe's biggest at that time. The new building was designed to mirror the exterior of Milan's La Scala and the interiors of the San Carlo in Naples. The theatre is the home of the National Opera Company. During the summer months an amazing open-air festival is held here, the Festival ao Largo.

329 FUNDAÇÃO GULBENKIAN

Av. de Berna 45-A
Avenidas Novas ⑧
+351 21 782 3000
www.gulbenkian.pt

Upon his death Calouste Gulbenkian, one of the world's richest men of his time, donated his full art collection and all his wealth to a foundation that bears his name, which then became the country's major private cultural institution. The Gulbenkian Foundation includes a world-class museum, an auditorium, and has its own orchestra.

330 TEATRO SÃO LUIZ

Rua António Maria Cardoso 38
Chiado ⑥
+351 21 325 7640
www.teatrosaoluiz.pt

Across the street from the São Carlos Theatre lies this other theatre, which is managed by the municipality. On the programme here you will find plays by mostly Portuguese playwrights, with a special focus on the work of more alternative theatre companies and young aspiring artists.

The 5 best
ART GALLERIES

———

331 CRISTINA GUERRA
Rua Santo António à
Estrela 33
Estrela ③
+351 21 395 9559
www.cristina
guerra.com

Opened in 2001 and led by Portugal's most international art gallerist, Cristina Guerra, this gallery represents several leading Portuguese contemporary artists (João Louro, Julião Sarmento) as well as some of the most sought after international names, like John Baldessari and Erwin Wurm.

332 FILOMENA SOARES
R. da Manutenção 80
Beato ⑨
+351 21 862 4122
www.gfilomena
soares.com

A regular guest at the best art fairs in the world, Galeria Filomena Soares is solely dedicated to contemporary art, showcasing regular exhibitions by the well-known Portuguese and international artists it represents. The gallery is located in the up-and-coming quarter Beato.

333 BAGINSKI
Rua Capitão
Leitão 51-53
Beato ⑨
+351 21 397 0719
www.baginski.com.pt

Andréa Baginski Champalimaud's gallery represents all kinds of contemporary artistic practices. In a former warehouse in Beato, Andréa shows the work of established as well as emerging artists, with a particular focus on Europe, Africa and Latin America.

334 VERA CORTÊS
Rua João Saraiva 16, 1°
Avenidas Novas ⑧
+351 21 395 0177
www.veracortes.com

Vera Cortês' art agency moved from Santos to a bigger space in Avenidas Novas, where she represents contemporary artists like Alexandre Farto (aka Vhils), Daniel Blaufuks and Gabriela Albergaria. With an extensive track record in Portugal, Vera Cortês has a more comprehensive approach than most galleries.

335 JOÃO ESTEVES DE OLIVEIRA
Rua Ivens 38
Chiado ⑥
+351 21 325 9940
www.jeogaleria.com

This is yet another case of an expert art collector who turned gallerist. João Esteves de Oliveira, a former banker, opened his gallery in Chiado in 2002 and opted to focus solely on works on paper by modern and contemporary Portuguese artists. Needless to say, his gallery is quite unique.

The 5 most intruiging
STATUES

336 MARQUÊS DE POMBAL
Praça do Marquês de Pombal
Av. da Liberdade ④

This statue is Lisbon's tribute to the resourceful and implacable marquis of Pombal, who was the prime minister at the time of the 1755 earthquake and later directed the city's urban renewal. He stands 40 metres high on top of a stone pedestal with a lion by his side.

337 D. PEDRO IV
Praça do Rossio
Baixa ⑥

The imposing bronze statue of King Pedro IV stands 27,5 metres high, ruling over the square of Rossio. Pedro was the 28th king of Portugal and also the first emperor of Brazil, which makes him a very unique figure in Portuguese history.

338 MATERNIDADE
Jardim Amália Rodrigues
Parque Eduardo VII ④

Most locals have no idea that Lisbon has a statue by leading Colombian artist Fernando Botero. This valuable public artwork depicting motherhood was made in 1989 and stands in the Amália Rodrigues garden, in the Edward the 7th park. It's a bronze piece and a great example of Botero's iconic artistic style.

339 LISBOA
Praça 25 de Abril
Beato ⑨

Lisboa was created by José de Guimarães, one of Portugal's leading contemporary artists, as an ode to the people who build cities. In red and green, the colours of the Portuguese flag, the statue shows a feminine figure leaning towards the river with her arms wide open.

340 D. JOSÉ I
Praça do Comércio
Baixa ⑥

Terreiro do Paço square has at its central point an equestrian statue of King José I, the monarch at the time of the 1755 earthquake. The bronze statue was designed by sculptor Machado de Castro. The king refused to pose for it, leaving the artist no choice but to rely solely on portraits.

340 D. JOSÉ I

5 special
PAINTINGS in the MUSEUM OF ANCIENT ART

MUSEU NACIONAL DE ARTE ANTIGA
Rua das Janelas Verdes
Santos ③
+351 21 391 2800
www.museudearteantiga.pt

341 TENTAÇÕES DE SANTO ANTÃO

This triptych by Hieronymus Bosch has the same theme as almost all of this artist's work: the temptation and loneliness of the just man when faced with evil and the diabolical. These forces that dominate the earthly world are depicted either explicitly, in the form of the monstrous and the hybrid, or under the guise of a false and provocative beauty.

342 PAINÉIS DE SÃO VICENTE

This is a work of highly symbolic importance in Portuguese culture. The paintings present a group of 58 people (representing the Court and various groups of Portuguese society at that time) gathered in an act of veneration directed towards St Vincent, the patron of the 15th-century military expansion into the Maghreb.

343 SÃO JERÔNIMO

This depiction of St Jerome by Dürer shows an innovation in the iconography and pictorial representation of the patron saint of Christian humanists. The 'Doctor of the Church' is represented by the powerful and synthetic image of an old sage, melancholically meditating on death and the contingency of the human condition.

344 SÃO AGOSTINHO

This painting was part of a polyptych by Piero della Francesca, made for the church at Borgo Sansepolcro. The painter's genius is evident in the solemn monumentality of the figure of the Saint (a characteristic feature of the Renaissance style), in the extraordinary simplicity of the construction of the pictorial space and also in the lively depiction of certain details.

345 SÃO PEDRO

This is the central painting of a series of 12 that together form an Apostolate, and it's the only one that is signed and dated by the artist. This group of paintings was destined for the monastery of the canons Regular of São Vicente de Fora. Their function was to affirm the unity of the dogma, as a symbol of the triumphant Church in a time when the Counter Reformation was still in progress.

5 of the most important
CONTEMPORARY
ARTISTS *in Lisbon*

346 JOÃO LOURO
www.joaolouro.com

João Louro studied architecture and painting, but his work also touches areas as diverse as photography, sculpture, and video installations. One of his concerns is, as he puts it, 'the reorganisation of the visual world and what visuality means'. In 2015 João Louro was the Portuguese national participant at the Biennale di Venezia.

347 JOANA VASCONCELOS
www.joana vasconcelos.com

Joana Vasconcelos is Portugal's most internationally recognised contemporary artist. Her work is based on the appropriation, decontextualisation and subversion of pre-existent objects and everyday realities, namely those of Portuguese popular culture. She has had exhibitions in venues like the Biennale di Venezia and the Château de Versailles.

348 **PEDRO CABRITA REIS**
www.pedro
cabritareis.com

Pedro Cabrita Reis is another one of the few Portuguese contemporary artists with an international reputation. His multi-platform oeuvre (painting, sculpture, photography, and installation) is characterised by an idiosyncratic, philosophical and poetical discourse that uses industrial, found materials and manufactured objects.

349 **JULIÃO SARMENTO**
www.julia
sarmento.com

Julião Sarmento has developed a multi-media visual language combining film, sound, painting, sculpture and installations, and his work deals with subjects like interpersonal relationships, sensuality, voyeurism and transgression.

350 **ALEXANDRE FARTO AKA VHILS**
www.alexandre
farto.com

Alexandre Farto is a contemporary artist who, as his alter ego Vhils, creates works that interact with the urban landscape. He has achieved international acclaim for the singularity and quality of his work, namely his dramatic, oversized portraits of ordinary people who he turns into icons. They are made by carving directly into the walls of buildings.

The 5 best places to see
AZULEJOS

---

351 MUSEU DO AZULEJO
Rua da Madre de
Deus 4
Beato ⑨
+351 21 810 0340
*www.museudo
azulejo.pt*

This national museum dedicated to glazed tiles showcases the evolution of this ancient form of art since its inception in ancient Egypt up to today. Set in a superb 15th-century convent decorated with *azulejos*, this museum is unique in its kind in the entire world.

352 PALÁCIO FRONTEIRA
Largo de São Domin-
gos de Benfica 1
Benfica ⑧
+351 21 778 2023
*www.fronteira-
alorna.pt*

This outstanding private palace, still owned by the Marquis of Fronteira, is known for its rich interiors, its French-style box garden and, above all, for its unique and magnificent collection of *azulejos*, that form a series of images dedicated to the Portuguese kings and to Greek and Roman mythology.

**353 CONVENTO DOS
CARDAES**
Rua do Século 123
Príncipe Real ⑤
+351 21 342 7525
*www.convento
doscardaes.com*

This nuns' convent, hidden in a quiet street of Príncipe Real, is still in operation. It holds a valuable series of glazed tile panels dating from the late 1600s. Using only white and blue, the panels were created by Dutch tile artist Jan van Oort. They depict the story of the convent's patron saint, Theresa of Avila.

354 VIDA PORTUGUESA (VIÚVA LAMEGO)

Largo do Intendente Pina Manique 23
Baixa ⑧
+351 21 346 5073
www.avida
portuguesa.com

The Viúva Lamego factory has been the most important glazed tile production facility in Portugal since 1849, specialising in the more delicate and artistic versions of this traditional wall covering material. Its former factory/shop in Intendent is in itself a jewel of the art of the *azulejos*, boasting a façade covered in beautifully coloured tiles.

355 CASA DO FERREIRA DAS TABULETAS

Largo Rafael Bordallo Pinheiro
Chiado ⑥

This iconic building in Chiado (one of the top photo spots in Lisbon) was built in 1864 and has a façade completely covered with decorative tiles produced at the Viúva Lamego factory. They show six allegorical figures representing Earth, Land, Water, Trade, Industry, Science and Agriculture.

351 MUSEU DO AZULEJO

The 5 most interesting places of
JEWISH HERITAGE

---

356 SINAGOGA
**Rua Alexandre
Herculano 59
Av. da Liberdade** ④
+351 21 393 1130
www.cilisboa.org

The Lisbon Synagogue Shaaré Tikvah
(Gates of Hope) dates from 1904. It was
the first synagogue to be built in Portugal
since the late 15th century, when the Jews
were expelled from the country. It was
designed by architect Ventura Terra in
a mix of the neo-byzantine and the neo-
romanesque style.

357 ALFAMA
**Rua da Judiaria
Alfama** ⑦

The street of the Jewish community in
Alfama (Rua da Judiaria) reminds us that
once there was a Jewish settlement here,
the history of which goes back as far as
the 13th century. A synagogue was built in
1373 but it was destroyed without leaving
any visible traces. There are some houses
that, however, still have doors with the
star of David engraved in them.

358 JEWISH CEMETERY
Rua Afonso III 44
Alto de São João ⑨

In 1868, by a royal decree, King Luís granted the Portuguese Jewish community the permission to create a cemetery to adequately bury its members. This is still the main Jewish burial ground in the city.

359 TERREIRO DO PAÇO
Baixa ⑥

In the 16th century this place was the scene of horrific ceremonies aimed against Jews, and led by the ruthless Holy Inquisition. These *autos-de-fé* ('acts of faith') were rituals during which condemned so-called 'heretics' were forced to do penance. Their punishment could go as far as execution by burning.

360 ROSSIO
Largo de São Domingos
Baixa ⑥

The Rossio square used to be the location of the headquarters of the Holy Inquisition, until it was abolished in 1821. Now the D. Maria National Theatre stands in its place. The adjoining square of São Domingos witnessed many *autos-de-fé*, including the horrific burning of live people. Not the best period in Portuguese history.

The 5 most beautiful
PAVEMENTS

361 **PADRÃO DOS DESCOBRIMENTOS**
Belém ②
*www.padraodos
descobrimentos.pt*

This is by far the city's most impressive cobblestone work. The gigantic mosaic on the footsteps of the Padrão dos Descobrimentos depicts a map of the world engulfed by an oversized compass that shows the routes of the Portuguese sea explorers. You will need to look down at it from the top of the monument to grasp its beauty.

362 **AV. DA LIBERDADE**
Av. da Liberdade ④

Av. da Liberdade, Lisbon's main thoroughfare, has some of the most noteworthy cobblestone pavements in the city. The oversized sidewalks are filled with floral designs. On the high end of the street, there's a star that's the crest of Lisbon, depicting two crows on a caravel, while down in Restauradores you can admire a pattern created by artist Abel Manta.

361 PADRÃO DOS DESCOBRIMENTOS

363 PARQUE DAS NAÇÕES
www.portal dasnacoes.pt

The tradition of creating cobblestone pavements is very much alive today in Lisbon, as can be seen in the modern district of Parque das Nações. This area was developed for the World Expo of 1998, which was dedicated to the Portuguese Discoveries, and so the designs were inspired by the oceans and depict sea monsters, mermaids, and other marine elements.

364 AMÁLIA BY VHILS
Rua de São Tomé Alfama ⑦

The famous Portuguese cobblestone pavements (*calçada à Portuguesa*) were the inspiration for an artwork created in Alfama by street artist Vhils. His tribute to legendary fado performer Amália Rodrigues shows her face on a wall, and the image flows over to the ground. It is both contemporary and traditional, and instantly became a new landmark in the city.

365 PRAÇA DO ROSSIO
Baixa ⑥

Rossio, the pivotal square in downtown Lisbon, is said to be the place where the art of decorating sidewalks and pavements with cobblestone designs emerged. Its wave-like pattern (the 'Wide Ocean') dates from the mid 1800s and was so popular that it was recreated in Rio de Janeiro in Brazil, where it became an iconic feature.

5 places to discover
FERNANDO PESSOA

---

366 CASA FERNANDO PESSOA
Rua Coelho da Rocha 16
Campo de Ourique ③
+351 21 391 3270
casafernandopessoa. cm-lisboa.pt

This municipal cultural centre occupies the house where the famous poet and writer spent the last few years of his life. The collection includes some of the author's personal objects, all of his literary works and secondary literature. There are regular events including seminars and poetry readings.

367 LARGO DE SÃO CARLOS
Largo de São Carlos
Chiado ⑥

Pessoa was born on the fourth floor of the building right across from the São Carlos National Theatre, where his father, who was a music critic, often worked. In 2008, on the celebration of the poet's 120th birthday, the municipality unveiled yet another bronze statue in his honour at this location.

368 LARGO DO CARMO
Largo do Carmo
Chiado ⑥

After having spent ten years of his life in the South African city of Durban, Pessoa returned to Lisbon where he rented a room immediately across from the ruins of the Carmo Convent. The apartment is now a Fernando Pessoa-themed guest house.

369 ESTÁTUA DO CHIADO

Largo do Chiado
Chiado ⑥

Fernando Pessoa was known to spend many of his days sitting on the terrace of Cafe A Brasileira in Chiado. To evoke that memory, a statue has been put up on the exact spot where he used to sit. The real-size figure is sitting, legs crossed, next to a table. A vacant chair next to him invites tourists to sit and take photos.

370 MARTINHO DA ARCADA

Praça do Comércio 3
Baixa ⑥
+351 21 887 9259
www.martinho
daarcada.pt

This iconic cafe in Terreiro do Paço is the oldest in Lisbon and another one of Pessoa's favourite places. He frequently enjoyed his meals here, up to his very last days, and he always sat at the same table, where he would write down his thoughts in poems and books.

370 MARTINO DA ARCADA

The 5 best places to hear
LIVE MUSIC

**371 LISBON LIVING
ROOM SESSIONS**
*lisbonlivingroom
sessions.blogspot.pt*

Joanna Hecker and Ricardo Lopes organise regular musical pop-up events in landmark houses around Lisbon, cordially opened by its owners. The events are always intimate and secret, as attendees have no clue about the location until a few hours before the event. They also run weekly jazz concerts in places like Rive Rouge.

**372 HOT CLUBE
DE PORTUGAL**
**Praça da Alegria 48
Av. da Liberdade ④
+351 21 361 9740
www.hcp.pt**

This bar is quite an institution in the Portuguese music scene. Opened in the mid-20th century, Hot Clube is on the list of the oldest jazz clubs in the world. It's a local and also an international reference and it has welcomed artists like Dexter Gordon and Quincy Jones.

373 TEMPLÁRIOS BAR

Rua Flores do Lima 8
Avenidas Novas ⑧
+351 21 797 0177
www.templarios.pt

Here is one of those gems that tend to stay unnoticed even by discerning locals, because most people seldom go out in this residential part of town. Open since 1991, this bar on Avenidas Novas hosts daily live music shows by amateur and garage bands, and also live stand-up comedy shows.

374 POPULAR ALVALADE

Rua António
Patrício 11-B
Alvalade ⑧
+351 21 796 0216
www.facebook.com/
PopularAlvalade

Popular is located off the main touristic quarters and is therefore a place almost exclusively visited by locals, that flock there for its regular live music shows. Performances are varied, including styles like rock, pop, world, indie and pop rock.

375 XAFARIX

Avenida Dom
Carlos I 69
Santos ③
+351 21 395 1395

Owned by members of the historic band Trovante, this is a traditional and intimate live music hangout that has been around since the late 80s. The bar gets its name from its location inside an old water reservoir that supplied residents with clean water (*chafariz*).

The 5 best
FILMS
set in Lisbon

---

376 NIGHT TRAIN TO LISBON

This movie by Billie August tells the story of Raimund Gregorius, a Swiss professor who saves a beautiful woman from committing suicide. In her coat, he finds the address of a bookstore, and there he comes across a book by a Portuguese writer, with a train ticket to Lisbon in it. Obsessed with the book, he decides to take the train to Lisbon to meet the author.

377 LISBON STORY

In this film by Wim Wenders, the main character, a movie director, comes to Lisbon and invites a sound engineer to record sounds for a film about the Portuguese capital. The movie shows the engineer wandering around the city recording the music of Lisbon and meeting interesting individuals as he goes along.

378 THE HOUSE OF SPIRITS

The House of Spirits isn't really a movie about Lisbon, but the city was used as a set for all the urban scenes, as if it were Santiago do Chile. The family estate of the Trueba family, the main characters in this saga, was artificially erected in southern Portugal so you can say that the country plays a big part in the movie.

379 ON HER MAJESTY'S SECRET SERVICE

Oddly enough, this 1969 James Bond movie (the only one starring George Lazenby) filmed in Portugal was not shown in the country until after the revolution of 1974, since the dictatorial regime didn't aprove its local screening. To the history of the Bond franchise remains the memory of his marriage and the death of his wife Teresa.

380 MYSTERIES OF LISBON

The nearly five-hour-long *Mysteries of Lisbon* tells the story of an orphan, Pedro da Silva, and his quest to find his true identity through a whirlpool of adventures and escapades, love affairs and crimes, woven in voyages around the world. The cast includes names like Ricardo Pereira, Maria João Bastos and Helena Coelho as the Marquise of Santa Eulália.

The 5 most unforgettable
FADO EXPERIENCES

---

381 ALFAMA
Alfama ⑦

Alfama lives and breathes fado; it's as if the whole neighbourhood moves to the slow pace of this melancholic tune that is the soul of Portugal. The local residents are immersed in fado from a tender age, and many of them grow up to be fado singers, guitar players or owners of fado restaurants.

382 MUSEU DO FADO
**Largo do Chafariz
de Dentro 1
Alfama** ⑦
+351 21 882 3470
www.museudofado.pt

As you could expect, the Museum of Fado is in Alfama. This cultural institution tells the story of fado and of the social environment the music thrives in. Available for listening are recordings that illustrate the different nuances in this music genre, namely the differences between fado from Lisbon or Coimbra, aristocratic or vagrant.

383 CIDADE DO FADO TRUCK
Rua do Carmo
Chiado ⑥

The air in the Rua do Carmo in Chiado is nearly always filled with the delicate sounds of Portuguese guitars and mellow voices, thanks to António Cardoso, the owner of the Cidade do Fado truck that since the 90s has never left this street. He is an expert connoisseur of fado and is a friendly resource for tourists looking for the right CD to buy.

384 CASA MUSEU AMÁLIA RODRIGUES
Rua São Bento 193
Príncipe Real ⑤
+351 21 397 1896
www.amalia
rodrigues.pt

Amália Rodrigues was to fado what the Beatles were to pop music. This stunningly beautiful and strong-minded world-famous diva was an icon during her lifetime and has been a goddess since her death. She was so relevant to Portuguese culture that she was buried in the National Pantheon. Her house is now a small museum where her personal items are on display.

385 REAL FADO
Príncipe Real ⑤
+351 21 340 4150
www.eastbanc.pt/
realfado

Real Fado celebrates the unique music genre of fado by organising weekly shows in different and surprising locations in Príncipe Real, some of which are unknown even to locals. Each venue's character is incorporated into the shows, with the following themes: Traditional, Fado & Other Sounds, Timeless Fado.

5 very exclusive
PRIVATE CLUBS

---

386 **TURF**
Rua Garrett 74
Chiado ⑥
+351 21 346 0975
www.turf-club.org

The Turf Club, aka the 'Society for the Improvement of Horse Breeds', is a private male members club located in Chiado, claiming to be the most exclusive club in Lisbon. It is one of the two aristocratic clubs in the city (the other is the 'Real Tauromáquico') and it prides itself more on the blood lines of its members than on its horses – there aren't any to be seen there.

387 **SOCIEDADE DE GEOGRAFIA**
Rua das Portas de Santo Antão 100
Av. da Liberdade ④
+351 21 342 5401
www.socgeografia lisboa.pt

Established in 1875 in an amazing building near Av. da Liberdade, the Lisbon Geographical Society was "aimed at promoting and assisting the study and progress of geography and related sciences". It was here that the explorers of Africa would come to present their findings. Today the society still has a cultural footprint.

388 GRÉMIO LITERÁRIO

Rua Ivens 37
Chiado ⑥
+351 21 347 5666
www.gremio
literario.pt

Founded under the patronage of Queen Maria the Second, this members club was always more socially tolerant than its Chiado neighbours Turf and Tauromáquico, welcoming intellectuals of both noble or common birth. It was at first also a sports club, but now it only has a literary and cultural agenda.

389 CLUBE TAUROMÁQUICO

Rua Ivens 72 1º
Chiado ⑥
+351 21 346 0973

The Royal Bullfighting Club was at its inception a club of bullfighting loving aristocrats. Rivaling with the Turf as far as Old World charm and anachronisms go, the Tauromáquico remains true to its original DNA: it's a private, by invitation only, exclusively male members club, and it will likely be so until the last remnants of that lifestyle die out.

390 CÍRCULO EÇA DE QUEIROZ

Largo Rafael Bordalo
Pinheiro 4
Chiado ⑥
+351 21 342 8758
www.circuloeca
dequeiroz.com

This social and intellectual club was founded in 1940 to promote literature and the arts through conferences, exhibitions and concerts, and has welcomed personalities like T.S. Eliot and Graham Greene. It's less elitist than the other clubs, and more concerned with the professional and social merit of its members than with their birth.

JARDIM DA ESTRELA

20 THINGS TO DO WITH CHILDREN

The 5 best places to take
SMALL CHILDREN

---

391 OCEANÁRIO

Esplanada Dom
Carlos I
Parque das Nações ⑩
+351 21 891 7000
www.oceanario.pt

This is one of the largest and most impressive sea aquariums in the world, with over 25.000 sea creatures living together (except for the sharks) in a huge tank – all the existing ocean habitats are there. It is a magnificent themed experience that dazzles children and adults alike.

392 ZOO

Praça Marechal
Humberto Delgado
Sete-Rios ⑧
+351 21 723 2900
www.zoo.pt

Lisbon's Zoo, which dates from 1905, has undergone significant upgrades in the last years and is now on the same level as some of the best international zoos, despite its relatively small size. It's a nice venue for families visiting Lisbon, especially thanks to one of its attractions, Dolphin Bay, where visitors can watch a dolphins and sea lions show.

393 **PLANETÁRIO**

Praça do Império
Belém ②
+351 21 097 7350
planetario.marinha.pt

Lisbon's Planetarium is a theatre built specifically to mirror the night sky and to offer an educational and entertaining experience that's all about the science of astronomy. It has a large dome-shaped screen onto which scenes in the sky are projected in a highly realistic manner, thanks to the use of a wide variety of technologies.

394 **BORBOLETÁRIO**

Rua da Escola
Politécnica 56-58
Príncipe Real ⑤
+351 21 392 1800
www.museus.ulisboa.
pt/borboletario

Inside the Botanical Garden of Príncipe Real you will find the first butterflies nursery to be opened to the public on the Iberian Peninsula. In this acclimatised greenhouse visitors can witness the different stages in the lifecycle of a butterfly. The resident butterflies include the largest European species: the Giant Peacock moth, the Old World swallowtail and the Monarch butterfly.

395 **KIDZANIA**

Dolce Vita Tejo
Shopping Center
Av. Cruzeiro Seixas 7
Loures
+351 21 154 5530
www.kidzania.pt

Kidzania is a themed park aimed at families with children from 3 to 15 years old. It recreates a city on a children's scale, so the young ones can pretend to be adults and go about their lives and routines, working, entertaining themselves and managing make-believe public and administration institutions.

The 5 best
ICE-CREAM SHOPS

---

396 PALETARIA

Rua Saraiva de
Carvalho 120-A
Campo de Ourique ③
+351 91 727 8943
www.paletaria.com

The fresh, frozen fruit, all-natural *paletas* (popsicles) are a must-eat for ice-cream addicts. These *paletas* are made of fresh fruit and nothing more – no dairy products, no artificial flavourings. Some of the flavours include strawberry, kiwi, peach, grape, pineapple and mint, and mango. They are to die for...

397 ARTISANI

Avenida Alvares
Cabral 65-B
Estrela ③
+351 21 397 6453
*www.artisani
gelado.com*

This is the flagship shop of the Artisani ice-cream chain, located close to Jardim da Estrela, and offering handmade ice creams in flavours that range from the more traditional ones to the exciting signature creations of the company's ice-cream chefs.

398 NANNARELLA

Rua Nova da
Piedade 68
Príncipe Real ⑤
+351 92 687 8553

This tiny artisanal Italian ice-cream shop in São Bento has been the talk of the town since it opened and started serving amazing ice creams (at a very, very reasonable price). The ice creams are served Roman-style by the Italian owners themselves, with a spatula instead of a scoop and optional whipped cream on top.

399 SANTINI

Rua do Carmo 9
Chiado ⑥
+351 21 346 8431
www.santini.pt

This Italian-style third generation ice-cream franchise had a very successful store in Cascais for over 50 years, so they decided to venture out and open more branches. The Chiado shop is their biggest in Lisbon and at any time of the year you will be able to choose from over 20 creamy all-natural flavours.

400 FRAGOLETTO

Rua da Prata 61
Baixa ⑥
+351 21 347 9472

This small independent Baixa ice-cream parlour rivals with the big guys in terms of quality. Its Italian-style ice creams are made with fresh seasonal fruits, and there are also options for vegans (made with soy) or for people who are lactose intolerant.

398 NANNARELLA

The 5 loveliest
SHOPS FOR KIDS

---

401 HOSPITAL DE BONECAS
Praça da Figueira 7
Baixa ⑥
+351 21 342 8574
www.hospital
debonecas.com

The 19th-century Hospital das Bonecas (Doll Hospital) is one of Lisbon's most spectacular shops, and was even considered 'one of the coolest toy stores in the world' by *Reader's Digest*. Besides a place where you can buy dolls, it's also a workshop dedicated to restoring them (plastic surgery, transplants, etc.).

402 TERESA ALECRIM
Amoreiras Shopping Center
Amoreiras ④
+351 21 383 3335
www.teresaalecrim.com

A family-owned shop that was created by Teresa Carrusca in 1981. They sell items inspired by Portugal's centuries-old home textile tradition. Their baby line includes blankets, bags, beds, skirts, and many other precious and handmade products.

403 MINI BY LUNA
Rua Dom Pedro V 56
Príncipe Real ⑤
+351 21 346 5161

A multi-brand concept store in Príncipe Real that sells lines for children, women and for the home, by brands like ba&sh, Leon & Harper, Bobo Choses and Babe & Tess. The shop itself is quite charming, with a delightful private garden in the back where you have a magnificent view of the city.

404 **PAPABUBBLE**

Rua da
Conceição 117-119
Baixa ⑥
+351 21 342 7026
www.papabubble.com

Located right next to one of tram 28's stops in Baixa, this small shop hides a world of sweetness behind its colourful façade. Here candy masters make chemical-free (but nonetheless extremely sweet) caramel candies by hand, using traditional recipes.

405 **CAMPO DE OURIQUE**

Campo de Ourique ③

The neighbourhood of Campo de Ourique is like a giant open-air shopping mall filled with children's clothes. There's a huge number of shops that cater to all budgets. If you have kids, don't miss out on this shopping opportunity.

403 MINI BY LUNA

The 5 most fun
PLAYGROUNDS

---

406 JARDIM DA ESTRELA
Praça da Estrela
Estrela ③
+351 21 397 4818

Jardim da Estrela is Lisbon's best family garden. It's surrounded by the elegant residential districts of Estrela, Lapa and Campo de Ourique, where more children seem to be living than anywhere else in the city – that explains the liveliness of the garden. The playground is large and has seating areas for parents to watch their kids having fun.

407 PARQUE DA SERAFINA
Estrada da Serafina
Monsanto

The children's park of Alto da Serafina is by far the biggest in the city. Located in the midst of nature in the Monsanto park, it offers a wide range of facilities. There are sport activities, playgrounds, a driving school for children and a picnic area.

408 JARDIM DAS AMOREIRAS
Praça das Amoreiras
Amoreiras ④

The playground in the garden of Amoreiras is very small, befitting of the scale of this intimate piece of nature. It's a nice place to have a rest while visiting the city. Parents can watch their kids playing from the very pleasant kiosk where good value drinks and light meals are served.

409 PARQUE DA QUINTA DAS CONCHAS

Avenida Eugénio de Andrade
Lumiar

This is the central park of northern Lisbon, taking up 24 hectares in total. It has a playground, a multi sports court, a forest area with hiking trails, a restaurant and a kiosk. Children of the neighbourhood enjoy the extensive lawns, perfect for playing in the open air.

410 JARDIM DO PRÍNCIPE REAL

Praça do Príncipe Real
Príncipe Real ⑤

The Príncipe Real district doesn't only appeal to grown-ups; there are activities for children too. The garden has a lovely playground in the shade, where parents who are visiting the city can let their kids play and take a well-deserved (and probably much-needed) rest after climbing up and down the nearby hills with strollers and baby slings.

406 JARDIM DA ESTRELA

PALACIO BELMONTE

25 PLACES
TO SLEEP

The 5 most
GLAMOROUS HOTELS

---

411 RITZ

Rua Rodrigo da
Fonseca 88
Parque Eduardo VII ④
+351 21 381 1400
www.fourseasons.com/
pt/lisbon

This hotel has been the city's epitome of luxury and grandeur since it was built in the 1950s to accommodate Europe's elite. Now managed by the Four Seasons hotel chain, the Ritz maintains all the charm of a stand-alone, family-owned hotel. Its modernist décor includes Art Deco elements and impressive works of art – be sure to admire the tapestries by Almada Negreiros.

412 PESTANA PALACE

Rua Jau 54
Alcântara ①
+351 21 361 5600
www.pestana.com/pt/
hotel/pestana-palace

The palace this hotel partially occupies was built in the 1800s by the country's wealthiest man, the Marquis of Valle-Flôr, and is classified as a national monument. Located in the residential quarter of Santo Amaro, its rooms surround a lush garden where a secluded pool offers a peaceful getaway inside the city.

413 **AVENIDA PALACE**

R. 1º de Dezembro 123
Av. da Liberdade ④
+351 21 321 8100
www.hotel
avenidapalace.pt

This traditional hotel, a genuine Lisbon landmark, was opened in 1892 at the confluence of two of Lisbon's main squares, Rossio and Restauradores. It was Lisbon's leading five-star palace hotel for many years, and it still has all of its Belle Époque charm and elegance. It's next door to the iconic Rossio train station.

414 **LAPA PALACE**

Rua do Pau de
Bandeira 4
Lapa ③
+351 21 394 9494
www.olissippo
hotels.com

Tucked away in the peaceful residential quarter of Lapa and surrounded by embassies of foreign countries, this grand hotel was formerly the palace of the Counts of Valenças. The 109 richly decorated rooms give out onto an exotic subtropical garden and boast magnificent views of the tiled roofs of the old city and of the river.

415 **VALVERDE**

Av. da Liberdade 164
Av. da Liberdade ④
+351 21 094 0300
www.valverdehotel.com

This intimate, classic and elegant five-star hotel in Av. da Liberdade offers discerning guests 25 beautifully appointed rooms. The atmosphere here is one of complete privacy – even the reception is hidden as you walk up the stairs from the street. The hotel has a stunning outdoor patio with a plunge pool and a terraced restaurant.

The 5 best
SMALL HOTELS

---

416 LE CONSULAT

Praça Luís de
Camões 22
Chiado ⑥
+351 21 242 7470
www.leconsulat.pt

Housed in the building that used to house the consulate of Brazil, this unique hotel boasts 20 spacious suites, decorated with important artworks by local artists. The cocktail bar is one of the coolest places in town to have a drink, thanks to the view over the lively square of Luís de Camões.

417 BRITÂNIA

Rua Rodrigues
Sampaio, 17
Av. da Liberdade ④
+351 21 315 5016
www.hotel-britania.com

The Britânia is housed in a historic building designed by the leading architect of his time, Cassiano Branco. The Art Deco decorative elements dating from 1944 are still very present in the hotel, which exudes an old world charm unmatched in Lisbon. Service is excellent and personal.

418 JANELAS VERDES

Rua das Janelas
Verdes 47
Lapa ③
+351 21 396 8143
www.asjanelas
verdes.com

This home-style hotel is set in a beautiful building from the 1800s where famous novelist Eça de Queiroz once lived. The terraced garden and library on the upper floor boast a surprising river view.

419 VERRIDE PALÁCIO DE SANTA CATARINA

Rua de Santa
Catarina 1
Santa Catarina ⑤
+351 21 157 3055
www.verridesc.pt

This stunning and intimate new hotel could very well be included in several categories of this book, given its palatial atmosphere, the stunning views from its rooms, and the sublime elegance of its décor. Located in the magical small quarter of Santa Catarina, on the edge of Bica and Bairro Alto, it stands high above the city, as if floating in its own heaven.

420 BAIRRO ALTO HOTEL

Praça Luís de
Camões 2
Chiado ⑥
+351 21 340 8288
www.bairroalto
hotel.com

This hotel, member of the Leading Hotels of the World, was the first of its kind to open its doors in Lisbon, setting the tone for the city's boutique hotels scene. The 55 rooms give out onto the busy square of Camões, the gateway to Bairro Alto, or to the Tagus river. The terrace is one of the city's best spots for a drink or a light meal.

The 5 best lodgings for a
ROOM WITH A VIEW

---

421 MEMMO ALFAMA

Tv. Merceeiras 27
Alfama ①
+351 21 049 5660
www.memmo
alfama.com

You probably won't notice this hotel as you pass by the street that leads from the Sé to the Castle, as it lies hidden in a narrow alley. You will be mesmerised by the view it offers over Alfama and the river, likely to be the best hotel view in town. The very attentive hotel staff is there to help guests experience the quaint neighbourhood.

422 HOTEL DO CHIADO

Rua Nova do
Almada 114
Chiado ⑥
+351 21 325 6100
www.hoteldochiado.pt

Located next-door to the Chiado shopping arcade, this hotel is one of the buildings designed by architect Álvaro Siza Vieira, and offers one of the best views in the city, especially from the top floor rooms that overlook the Castle. These rooms have delightful outdoor terraces where guests can enjoy the picture-perfect scenery.

423 PALÁCIO CAMÕES

Largo do Calhariz 16-A
Chiado ⑥
+351 93 666 6600
www.palacio
camoes.com

This National Monument is one of the most iconic buildings in Lisbon. Located next to the Bica funicular and in the centre point of the city's golden triangle – Chiado, Bairro Alto and Santa Catarina – it was once the residence of the Marquis of Pombal and of President Sidónio Pais. The palace now houses ten apartments that offer amazing views on the city and the river.

424 TOREL PALACE

Rua Câmara
Pestana 23
Av. da Liberdade ④
+351 21 829 0810
www.torelpalace.com

Offering only ten suites, this gem of a hotel is located next to the Torel garden, on the highest end of Av. da Liberdade. Decorated in a classic-contemporary style, its highlight is the infinity pool perched over the city. It's a secluded oasis that is sure to charm guests with its private atmosphere.

425 BEAUTIQUE HOTEL FIGUEIRA

Praça da Figueira 16
Baixa ⑥
+351 21 049 2940
www.thebeautique
hotels.com

Occupying a reconverted 1800s building in the heart of downtown, this 50-room 'beautique' hotel, decorated by award-winning designer Nina Andrade Silva, offers impressive views of the castle hills below. The square, located between Rossio and Martim Moniz, is vibrant and lively every day of the week.

5

UNUSUAL PLACES TO SLEEP

---

426 PALÁCIO BELMONTE

Pátio de Dom
Fradique 14
Castelo ⑦
+351 21 881 6600
www.palacio
belmonte.com

Palácio Belmonte stands out in the Lisbon hotel scene, and deserves a class of its own. It's a secluded place, hidden behind an imposing gate by the castle walls, and offering 11 magnificent suites, all with impressive views of the old city. The palace itself dates from the 1500s and was renovated with care by Fréderic Coustols, its French owner. It has a cosy garden with a pool.

427 PALACETE CHAFARIZ D'EL REI

Tv. do Chafariz
del Rei 6
Alfama ⑦
+351 21 888 6150
www.chafarizdelrei.com

This is yet another Lisbon palace that was converted to high-end accommodations after first undergoing a profound renovation to restore all of its past grandeur. The architecture is neo-Moorish – a very fashionable style in the 1900s. The existing six suites are all different but share a common charming, discreet and luxurious feel.

428 THE KEEP – SLEEP BOUTIQUE/ PENSAO NINHO DE AGUIAS

Costa do Castelo 74
Castelo ⑦
+351 21 885 4070
www.thekeep-
lisbon.com

It's hard to match the view from this small 16-room hotel perched high above Lisbon, just below the Castle walls. It's not your traditional hotel, the feel here is more like that of a private residence where the owner personally welcomes guests and takes care of their stay. The building itself dates from 1885 and has been a hotel since the late 50s.

429 PALÁCIO RAMALHETE

Rua das Janelas
Verdes 92
Lapa ③
+351 21 393 1380
www.palacio-
ramalhete.com

This palace located in front of the National Ancient Art Museum is said to be the setting of one of Portugal's most famous novels, *The Maias*. The exclusive hotel has only 12 rooms and suites, installed in the manor house's living quarters. In the back there is an intimate garden with a small pool.

430 THE LATE BIRDS

Travessa André
Valente 21-21A
Bairro Alto ⑤
+351 93 300 0962
www.thelatebirds
lisbon.com

This charming and gay-friendly hotel lies a bit hidden in the heart of one of the trendiest areas of the city, on the edge of Bairro Alto and Santa Catarina. After you enter its discreet door you will find four floors with twelve beautifully decorated rooms, an idyllic pool and a lounge bar.

The 5 best
HOSTELS

---

431 THE INDEPENDENT

Rua de São Pedro
de Alcântara 83
Chiado ⑥
+351 21 346 1381
www.the
independente.pt

This hostel occupies two old mansions facing Lisbon's top viewpoint, the São Pedro de Alcântara garden, on the intersection of Chiado, Bairro Alto and Príncipe Real – undisputedly the best location in town. Here you will find dormitory style rooms and also four suites for more affluent guests.

432 LISBOA LOUNGE HOSTEL

Rua São Nicolau 41
Baixa ⑥
+351 21 346 2061
www.lisbonlounge
hostel.com

Winner of *The Times*' award for the 'best boutique hostel in the world', this hostel highly exceeds the expectations most people have of this type of lodging. The décor is upscale and makes the most of the character of the building where it is located. The hostel's lounge area is where everything happens.

433 LISB'ON HOSTEL

Rua do Ataíde 7-A
Baixa ⑥
+351 21 346 7413
lisb-onhostel.com

This hostel in Santa Catarina (owned by a well-established hotel group) is one of the world's best, offering fabulous views and an elegant décor. It has a terrace overlooking the river and public spaces for guests to socialise while having a drink or playing a game of pool.

434 HOME LISBON

Rua São Nicolau 13
Baixa ⑥
+351 21 888 5312
www.homelisbon
hostel.com

As far as a family and homely feel goes, this hostel is hard to beat – even the meals here are prepared by the owner's mother. Housed in a building from the 1800s, it has large rooms with private balconies, a cosy living and dining room, and even an outdoor area where you can enjoy the sun.

435 LISBON DESTINATION HOSTEL

Largo do Duque
de Cadaval 17
Baixa ⑥
+351 21 346 6457
destinationhostels.com

This highly original and memorable hostel is housed inside the 19th-century Rossio train station, one of the city's most iconic buildings. Occupying a renovated area of the station, it offers dormitory rooms and a winter garden. The hostel regularly hosts events and activities like DJ performances and movie nights.

431 THE INDEPENDENT

GUINCHO

45 WEEKEND ACTIVITIES

The 5 best
SUMMER FESTIVALS

---

436 NOS ALIVE
www.nosalive.com

This fantastic music festival, perhaps the largest yearly festival to take place in Portugal, attracts over 100.000 people and lasts three days. The line-up is formed by popular international bands, some of them very famous. The past editions welcomed the likes of Pearl Jam, Smashing Pumpkins, Metallica and the Black Eyed Peas.

437 OUT JAZZ
www.ncs.pt/ outjazz.php

More than a jazz festival, Out Jazz is a celebration of music in the outdoors. The festival is held over a five-month period, with concerts every Saturday and Sunday from May to September, in nice locations such as parks, squares and viewpoints all around Lisbon. The music is mostly jazz, performed live, but you can also listen to good local DJs performing here. Entrance is free.

438 EDP COOL JAZZ FEST
www.edpcooljazz.com

This high-quality festival is held in Oeiras, a seaside suburb of Lisbon, in two locations: one is the garden of a stunning 18th-century palace (for the more intimate concerts), the other is a football stadium (for larger events). It's a more upscale festival than the others and it tends to attract an older crowd.

439 FESTIVAL AO LARGO
www.festivalaolargo.pt

Festival ao Largo translates to 'Festival on the Square', so it's no surprise that it takes place on a square, more precisely on the small square right in front of the São Carlos theatre in Chiado. It gets filled to the brim with music lovers who come to enjoy classical music performances by leading Portuguese symphonic orchestras, choirs and opera singers.

440 CAIXA ALFAMA
www.caixaalfama.pt

This very original festival with no less than ten different pop-up stages in Alfama welcomes the biggest names in fado, and also some lesser-known amateur singers – more than 40 artists in total.

5 interesting
GUIDED TOURS

---

441 TASTE OF LISBOA
+351 91 560 1908
www.tasteoflisboa.com

Filipa Valente personally guides her guests on delicious walks around some of Lisbon's most interesting neighbourhoods, food-wise of course. The tours are very informative and take guests to places they would never dream of discovering if they were left on their own.

442 TUK TUK LISBOA
www.tuk-tuk-lisboa.pt

If you walk around Lisbon's most touristic quarters you will see dozens of tuk-tuks carrying visitors back and forth. These funny carts are a great way to visit the city, especially because their drivers are well-educated, friendly and knowledgeable about the history and traditions of Lisbon and its local population.

443 GOCAR

**Rua dos
Douradores 16
Baixa ⑥
+351 21 096 5030**
www.gocartours.com

GoCar is a 'GPS-guided storytelling car' that can be rented and driven around the city, to explore its less known corners. This car goes where normal cars often can't go, and the GPS system makes sure the clients/drivers can't get lost in the city, while also providing information about the monuments and sights.

444 SEGWAY TOURS

**Campo das Cebolas 21
Sé ⑦
+351 91 300 8027**
*www.lisbon
segwaytours.pt*

Unconventional tours with fun vehicles and fun tour guides – the latter are energetic, very communicative and know the city like the palms of their hands. It's a fun ride and it will not only test your riding skills, but also give you thrills.

445 LISBON HELICOPTERS

+351 21 301 1794
*www.lisbon
helicopters.com*

Lisbon is one of the most beautiful cities in the world and there is no better way to discover all of its splendour than by looking at it from the air. So go ahead and get into a helicopter that will fly you over the old city, alongside the river, past the 25th of April bridge and up to the mouth of the Tagus, where the river flows into the wide open sea. It's the experience of a lifetime.

The 5 best places to
PARTY AFTER DARK

---

446 BAIRRO ALTO
Bairro Alto ⑤

Bairro Alto still is in pole position as far as Lisbon nightlife is concerned, and it has by far the largest concentration of bars in town. The streets of this old quarter are always busy, thanks to bar-hopping youngsters, chatting and drinking in a very easy-going and relaxed way.

447 CAIS DO SODRÉ
Cais do Sodré ⑥

This once shabby area in the old town turned chic in just a year. It now is the most vibrant and coolest nightlife district, with new bars and restaurants popping up every month. The hub of it all is Pink Street (Rua Cor de Rosa), where the most popular bars are located. The nearby Mercado da Ribeira is a great option for dinner before the partying starts.

448 PRÍNCIPE REAL
Príncipe Real ⑤

Príncipe Real is many things, and one of them is a nightlife district, especially as far as restaurants are concerned. Bars here tend to close sooner than in neighbouring Bairro Alto. Nevertheless, the streets going down to Praça das Flores have a few nice spots for a drink (several of them targeting the gay community) that generally attract an older crowd than the bars in Bairro Alto.

449 ALCÂNTARA
Alcântara ①

The quarter of Alcântara has been a nightlife destination since the 80s. It still is the place to be if you want to go dancing in a club. As far as the bar scene is concerned, the options are rather limited, but the opening of LX Factory gave this area a boost, since it's a great place to start the night before venturing out to the party spots.

450 AVENIDA 24 DE JULHO
Santos ⑦

24 de Julho is a wide thoroughfare that borders the railway tracks and the river. On both sides of it there are plenty of bars and clubs, namely the well-known Main, Kais, Urban Beach, Meninos do Rio or B.Leza. There are countless options to party, no matter your age, lifestyle or musical preference.

5 places to
MEET NEW PEOPLE

---

451 RUA COR DE ROSA
Rua Nova do Carvalho
Cais do Sodré ⑥

'Pink Street' is Lisbon's top spot if you're looking to meet new people, both locals and visitors. This small street is home to a number of hip bars that get full easily, and so people just linger outside on the street talking and having drinks. On weekend nights the street is packed but the mood is always relaxed, fun and very safe.

452 PARK
Bairro Alto ⑤

This must be one of the best ideas of the last years in Lisbon: turn the rooftop of a car park into a bar with a great view over the old city and the river. It has a small indoor area and a large terrace with trees in pots. People sit outside enjoying the scenery and the mood is very light and fun.

453 QUIOSQUE DO OLIVEIRA
Praça do Príncipe Real
Príncipe Real ⑤

This tiny kiosk on the corner of the Príncipe Real garden is really something. It's very popular with BCBG locals, who flock to it on late afternoons to have a drink after work or before going out for dinner in the neighbourhood.

454 CHAPITÔ

Costa do Castelo 1
Castelo ⑦
+351 21 885 5550
www.chapito.org

Chapitô is a very interesting and well-rounded cultural institution dedicated to the circus arts. The school's restaurant and bar are very popular among locals and international visitors. They come for the stunning views of the city, the school's edgy cultural activities and the well-priced food and drinks.

455 MERCADO DA RIBEIRA

Avenida 24 de
Julho 50
Cais do Sodré ⑥

The renovated Mercado da Ribeira is unarguably Lisbon's main meeting point. Open every day of the week, the Mercado is the 'home away from home' of international visitors to the city. They go there to enjoy the many choices in food and beverages and to socialise with locals and other visitors, sitting at the long communal tables.

453 **QUIOSQUE DO OLIVEIRA**

The 5 best places for
CONCERTS

456 **AULA MAGNA**
   Almada da
   Universidade
   Av. Prof. Gama
   Pinto 3
   Avenidas Novas ⑧
   +351 21 011 3406
   www.aulamagna.pt

This is the amphitheatre of the University of Lisbon, where the university's events take place but also other happenings, mostly of a musical nature. It's located in the university's open campus, near Campo Grande, and seats 1653 spectators, making it one of the largest in town.

457 **GULBENKIAN**
   Avenida de Berna 45-A
   Avenidas Novas ⑧
   +351 21 782 3000
   www.gulbenkian.pt

The *grande auditório* of the Calouste Gulbenkian Foundation was built in 1969 to host the Foundation's diverse cultural events. With a maximum capacity of 1228 seats, the auditorium is primarily used for concerts by symphonic orchestras or chamber orchestras and for small group recitals, but it's also fit for plays, dance shows and opera.

458 CCB

**Praça do Império
Belém ②
+351 21 361 2400
www.ccb.pt**

The main auditorium of the Centro Cultural de Belém is the city's largest and it regularly presents world-class music, dance and theatre performances, offering the best cultural programming in town. Especially noteworthy are the annual springtime Dias da Música (Music Days) when there are several classical music concerts to be enjoyed by everyone.

459 MEO ARENA

**Rossio dos Olivais
Parque das Nações ⑩
Lote 2.13.01 A
+351 21 891 8409
www.meoarena.pt**

This venue by the river in Parque das Nações is where the biggest concerts and events take place. With a capacity of no less than 15.000 spectators, it has welcomed artists like Madonna, Lady Gaga, Coldplay and Rihanna. The arena has also hosted sports events like the Tennis Masters championships, and even a NATO World Summit.

460 COLISEU DOS RECREIOS

**Rua das Portas de
Santo Antão 96
Av. da Liberdade ④
+351 21 324 0580
www.coliseulisboa.com**

The magnificent Coliseu dos Recreios was built in the late 1800s to host large events. More than 100 years later it's still alive and kicking, hosting music, circus and theatre shows and also political and social events and galas. It can hold up to 7.000 spectators.

5 nice
DAY TRIPS

---

461 MAFRA

A 30-minute drive (by highway) will take you from Lisbon to Mafra where you can visit the magnificent 900-room royal palace and convent (and royal hunting grounds) that were built in 1717 by King João V to commemorate the birth of his daughter.

462 SINTRA

This hilltop village, a UNESCO World Heritage site, is filled with fairytale palaces, castles, lush gardens and magnificent viewpoints. The top sites include the palaces of Pena, Monserrate, Vila and Regaleira. It's also a mystical place, where, according to legend, the Celts worshipped the moon.

463 CASCAIS

The leisurely drive (or train ride) to Cascais (and its neighbouring village Estoril) runs alongside the river and the sea: here is one of the most beautiful scenic routes in the world. It's a perfect destination for a day at the beach, a seafood meal, a stroll on the boardwalk, or some shopping.

464 **ARRÁBIDA**

The scenic roads of the Arrábida mountain range boast dramatic views of the mountains dropping down to the blue sea, the white sand beaches, the Tróia peninsula and the mouth of the Sado river. It's indescribably beautiful. In Azeitão there are excellent wine and cheese tastings.

465 **ÉVORA**

The capital of the Alentejo region is inland Portugal's top destination. A UNESCO World Heritage Site, the city is very pleasant to walk around and getting lost along the way. The main interest points include the Roman temple of Diana, the Cadaval Palace, the cathedral, the Giraldo square and the Chapel of Bones.

462 **SINTRA**

The 5 most beautiful
LISBON AREA
BEACHES

---

466 GUINCHO

This usually pretty windy beach (it's popular with wind and kite surfers) is the most beautiful of the Lisbon and Cascais coastline, with the Sintra hills and the dunes serving as a natural backdrop. There is a more secluded part to the right.

467 COSTA DA CAPARICA

Across the Tagus lies the coastal resort village of Costa da Caparica, the *Lisboetas*' favourite beach destination. Each beach has its own feel and most of them have great beach bars and seafood restaurants. The best beaches are São João, Morena and Sereia.

468 MECO

This wide open beach is a favourite among local families but on its edges there are stretches that have traditionally been nudist spots. The famous Bar do Peixe serves amazing fish and seafood and organises fun sunset parties in summertime.

469 **ADRAGA**

People go to Adraga for the beauty of the scenery (a pristine sandy beach protected from the wind by its high cliffs), the fantastic fish restaurant (try the grilled fish, the *percebes* and the *bruxas*) and the fact that it is rarely too crowded. The nearby village of Almoçageme has a cute weekend farmers market.

470 **PORTINHO DA ARRÁBIDA**

Many people call this the most beautiful beach in Portugal. The main assets of this beach, adequately named 'Arrábida's Little Port' are the colour of its crystal-clear water and the Natural Park as the backdrop. There are limited parking places farther away from the beach so be prepared to walk a bit.

466 **GUINCHO**

The 5 best
SMALL CINEMAS
and THEATRES

---

471 CINEMA IDEAL
Rua do Loreto 15-17
Chiado ⑥
+351 21 099 8295
www.cinemaideal.pt

This 1904 movie theatre is the oldest in Lisbon. It was recently renovated but it hasn't lost its original neighbourhood feel. More than just a cinema, Cinema Ideal is a non-mainstream cultural venue (also open to other arts) that tries to program movies that are either independent or classic. This is the place to go for the oldies that are rarely shown in the standard cinemas.

472 LISBON PLAYERS
Rua da Estrela 10
Estrela ③
+351 21 396 1946
www.lisbon
players.com.pt

The Lisbon Players' Theatre occupies Estrela Hall, a 1906 building. It's an intimate theatre that's also the home of the amateur theatre company of the same name, the only one in Lisbon to perform an exclusively English repertoire, which they have been doing since the mid 20th century.

473 A BARRACA

Largo de Santos 2
Santos ⑦
+351 21 396 5360
www.abarraca.com

The A Barraca theatre company was founded in 1975 and was part of a generation of independent experimental theatre groups that emerged in Portugal in the post-revolution period. The company uses the Cinearte Theatre in Santos, a modernist and industrial-looking building from the 1930s, that also hosts other initiatives, like tango sessions.

474 TEATRO DO BAIRRO

Rua Luz Soriano 63
Bairro Alto ⑤
+351 21 347 3358
www.teatrodo
bairro.org

This theatre occupies a former printing facility. It's not a traditional theatre, in fact its programming is made up of edgy alternative plays, music concerts, parties and independent movie screenings.

475 CINEMATECA

Rua Barata
Salgueiro 39
Av. da Liberdade ④
+351 21 359 6200
www.cinemateca.pt

Cinemateca is Lisbon's Museum of Cinema, a state-owned cultural institution that guards Portugal's cinema heritage. The almost daily screenings here range from Portuguese films to foreign classics and independent films. There are also regular themed movie festivals.

The best 5 places for an
OUTDOOR RUN

---

476 TAGUS BOARDWALK
Belém ②

What better place to go for a jog than the 10-kilometre riverside boardwalk that runs alongside the Tagus from Terreiro do Paço up to Belém? The scenery is overwhelming and along the way there are many interesting points like the docks, the Electricity Museum, the Padrão dos Descobrimentos and the Tower of Belém.

477 PAREDÃO

This boardwalk runs from Paço de Arcos up to Cascais, alongside the sea. If offers a stunning scenery and it allows sports enthusiasts to enjoy the sea breeze and the beach during their workout. There are many restaurants and cafes for pit stops.

478 CAMPO GRANDE
Avenidas Novas ⑧

This 19th-century urban park was recently renovated and now offers picnic areas, kids' playgrounds, sports facilities, several paddle tennis courts, a restaurant, a lake with row boats and a running track where joggers can run in an urban but at the same time green setting.

479 **ESTÁDIO NACIONAL**
Algés ①

Estádio Nacional, also referred to as 'Jamor', is Portugal's national stadium and sports complex. It occupies an extensive plot of land on the edge of town and it boasts a football stadium, several rugby and football fields, a tennis club, a golf academy and extensive running tracks.

480 **MONSANTO**
Monsanto

This city forest is one of the largest in the world (over 1000 hectares) and offers a multitude of jogging opportunities, on all types of soil, from asphalt to gravel. There are dozens of kilometres of tracks in the middle of the forest also that attract trail runners and BMX riders.

476 TAGUS BOARDWALK

FERNANDO PESSOA

20 GOOD-TO-KNOW FACTS AND URBAN DETAILS

The 5 most famous people
BORN IN LISBON

---

481 FERNANDO PESSOA

Portugal's most celebrated modern writer and poet was born in Lisbon in 1888. He also wrote in English after having spent part of his childhood in South Africa. He wrote (and published) under his own name but he also had several pseudonyms, fictional characters in fact, with different literary styles; just one of the many elements that illustrate his genius and talent.

482 AMÁLIA RODRIGUES

There is no music rival to Amália Rodrigues in Portugal and there probably never will be. This iconic fado diva was born in Lisbon to a low class family and rose to stardom thanks to her voice, her stunning looks and her strong personality. She sang all over the world, taking Portugal's name and traditions everywhere. She was buried in the National Pantheon.

483 LUÍS VAZ DE CAMÕES   Camões is the author of the famous epic poem *The Lusiads*, published in 1572. It's a poetic and mythological narrative of Portuguese history and of Vasco da Gama's trip to India. Camões himself was an adventurer and spent time in India and Macao. He is regarded as one of the greatest poets of all times.

484 SANTO ANTÓNIO   Lisbon-born Saint Anthony was a scholar and a credited theologist who lived in the 13th century. Later in his life he moved to Italy, to the city of Padova, and he became known as Saint Anthony of Padova. He is traditionally seen as a matchmaker and during the city's June festival there it's tradition for the brides of Saint Anthony to get married in a group ceremony.

485 THE MARQUIS OF POMBAL   The first Marquis of Pombal was an 18th-century statesman who served as prime minister under King José the First. Under his reign Lisbon suffered a major earthquake that nearly destroyed the city completely. Pombal is regarded highly for showing leadership in the aftermath of the catastrophe and also for being a strong reformist. (Sometimes too strong actually; he was cruel to his enemies.)

5 of the best
LISBON ARCHITECTS

---

486 AIRES MATEUS
www.airesmateus.com

Brothers Manuel and Francisco Aires Mateus, who are at the helm of the architectural firm that bears their family name, are the two leading post-revolution architects in Portugal. Their extensive list of realisations includes many buildings in Lisbon, namely the new EDP Headquarters and the Rectory of the Universidade Nova de Lisbon.

487 GONÇALO BYRNE
www.byrnearq.com

Born in 1941, Gonçalo Byrne is one of the most awarded contemporary architects in Portugal. He is also an Architecture professor at the prestigious Harvard University. The tower he designed to house the maritime traffic coordination and control centre is already a landmark in the city and will grant him architectural immortality in Lisbon.

488 CARRILHO DA GRAÇA
www.jlcg.pt

João Luís Carrilho da Graça has worked on and is still working on many architecture projects in Lisbon, residential as well as commercial and public. His most relevant buildings include the Orient Museum, the Pavilion of the Knowledge of the Seas, the German School of Lisbon and the future cruise terminal.

489 MANUEL SALGADO
www.risco.org

Currently he is the number two of the municipality in charge of Urbanism, but before that Manuel Salgado was a partner at the successful architecture firm Risco. During that time he designed several important buildings around the city, among which are the Belém Cultural Center (with architect Vittorio Gregotti), Hotel Altis Belém and public spaces in Parque das Nações.

490 ÁLVARO SIZA VIEIRA
www.alvarosiza vieira.com

He isn't really from Lisbon – he was born in Porto – but nevertheless Pritzker Prize winner Álvaro Siza Vieira operates mostly in Lisbon. Some of his creations in the city have gained international acclaim; that's the case for the iconic Pavilion of Portugal and for restoration of the Chiado quarter after it had been severely damaged by a fire.

5 *important days in*
LISBON'S HISTORY

---

491 CONQUEST OF LISBON

Lisbon was once the capital of the Moorish regime that ruled the territory that is now Portugal. The military action during which the city was won back from the Moors is known as the Siege of Lisbon, and is considered one of the few military successes of the Second Crusade. The siege lasted from July 1st to October 25th 1147, and it played a pivotal role in the reconquest of Portugal.

492 1.1.1640

Portugal was under Spanish rule from 1380 to 1640, but on December 1st 1940, 40 aristocratic rebels under the command of the Duke of Bragança stormed into the king's palace and killed his secretary of state. They immediately proclaimed the Duke king, John the Fourth, in front of the eyes of Lisbon's cheering population.